THE UNIVERSITY, THE CITIZEN, AND WORLD AFFAIRS

Studies in
Universities and World Affairs—

AMERICAN COLLEGE LIFE AS EDUCATION IN WORLD OUTLOOK
Howard E. Wilson

FOREIGN STUDENTS AND HIGHER EDUCATION
IN THE UNITED STATES
Cora Du Bois

THE UNIVERSITY, THE CITIZEN, AND WORLD AFFAIRS
Cyril O. Houle and Charles A. Nelson

WORLD AFFAIRS AND THE COLLEGE CURRICULUM
Vincent Baker

TRAINING OF SPECIALISTS IN INTERNATIONAL RELATIONS
C. Dale Fuller

UNIVERSITY RESEARCH ON WORLD AFFAIRS
John Gange

WORLD AFFAIRS IN INSTITUTIONS OF HIGHER EDUCATION
IN THE SOUTH
Fred Cole and Richard W. Sterling

AMERICAN UNIVERSITIES IN WORLD AFFAIRS:
A GENERAL REPORT
Howard E. Wilson

THE UNIVERSITY, THE CITIZEN, AND WORLD AFFAIRS

CYRIL O. HOULE

CHARLES A. NELSON

AMERICAN COUNCIL ON EDUCATION · *Washington, D. C.*

Prepared fo. ... ... g ... owment for International Peace, the Adult Education Association of the U.S.A., the Association of University Evening Colleges, and the National University Extension Association; published by the American Council on Education

© 1956 by Carnegie Endowment for International Peace
United Nations Plaza at 46th Street
New York 17, New York

LIBRARY OF CONGRESS CATALOG CARD NO. 56-13172

PRINTED IN THE UNITED STATES OF AMERICA

To
George W. Overton

Foreword

THIS COMPREHENSIVE treatment of the role of the university in educating adults about world affairs is the product of a long and fruitful collaboration. We who sign this Foreword do so on behalf of the four official sponsors of the volume, but a brief history of how it came into being demonstrates the fact that many other institutions, associations, and individuals have also been involved.

The original impetus came from the Carnegie Endowment for International Peace. As Dr. Howard Wilson makes clear in the Preface, the Endowment had long been concerned with the education in world affairs provided by colleges and universities for mature citizens, and in 1953 decided to include a treatment of this subject in the series of volumes which it was then planning. The Adult Education Association was invited to serve as cosponsor and enthusiastically accepted. Its leaders recognized the significance of the subject for the development of university policy and for the strengthening of the adult educational movement.

The two authors selected by the Endowment and the Association have had long experience in the general field covered by this book. Cyril O. Houle has been actively engaged in adult education since 1935, and, since 1939, has taught graduate courses in that subject at the University of Chicago. From 1944 to 1953 he was also the dean of University College, the adult educational division of the university. He has had two periods of extended study and observation in Europe, has served as the director of an international seminar on adult education sponsored by Unesco, and has lectured at the Universities of Stockholm, Cambridge,

Leeds, and Birmingham. He was selected by Unesco to write the introduction to its comparative study of university adult education and has participated in many other conferences on that subject both in the United States and abroad. Charles A. Nelson served as assistant to the president at St. John's College and was also for a period of years the director of the Basic Program of Liberal Education for Adults at the University of Chicago. From 1947 to 1956,[1] as executive director of the American Foundation for Political Education, he was responsible for the development and nation-wide expansion of its courses in world politics.

Mr. Houle and Mr. Nelson, when asked to undertake the assignment of preparing the present volume, suggested that in the course of collecting data, they would like to try to develop the field of world affairs education for adults even further and that this result might be brought about by involving in their study a number of university presidents, deans, and other officials. The funds then available would not have permitted the extensive travel, conferences, and other means necessary to bring about this result. The Adult Education Association accordingly sought and obtained a grant from the Carnegie Corporation of New York which, added to the funds provided by the Carnegie Endowment, made this expanded program possible.

The Endowment and the Adult Education Association then invited the Association of University Evening Colleges and the National University Extension Association to join with them in the cosponsorship of the study. The acceptances were immediate and enthusiastic.

The process used by the authors in compiling this volume has without doubt produced many desirable results, even before publication. In the course of many conferences and interviews, leading university officers have been stimulated to fresh thought, to re-examination of policies, and to new insights concerning world affairs education for adults. The publication of the study should,

---

[1] Mr. Nelson is now a management consultant with the firm of Cresap, Mc-Cormick and Paget.

however, extend this influence greatly. University presidents, deans, trustees, and faculty members will now have available the fruits of most incisive thinking about long-run directions for the development of university policy in this important area of social concern.

All the undersigned, on behalf of their organizations, bear witness to the competence of the authors and the effectiveness of the process they used in making the study. The product is, in our estimation, an example of educational statesmanship of the highest order. The authors themselves—and not the Endowment, the three associations, and the Carnegie Corporation—are responsible, of course, for the statements made and the views which they have expressed.

JOSEPH E. JOHNSON, President, Carnegie Endowment
for International Peace

KENNETH BENNE, President, Adult Education
Association of the U.S.A.

GEORGE PARKINSON, President, Association of
University Evening Colleges

ROY R. TOMPKINS, President, National University
Extension Association

Editor's Preface

SINCE THE BEGINNING of the twentieth century American colleges and universities have been increasingly influenced by world affairs and by the rising importance of foreign policy and international relations for the United States. Under the impact of international developments there have been extensive changes in the curricula of higher education, of which the rise of courses in international law and organization and politics is only one part. World area studies have been organized, and the internationally comparative approach has affected every field, from public administration to literature. Colleges have lost their students during periods of war, and veterans have left their mark on postwar college life. Great numbers of foreign students have arrived. Extensive research programs on international relations and on the means of national defense have been undertaken by universities. Hardly an aspect of academic life has escaped the influence of world events and movements. And the changes which have occurred or are now in process seem certain to be followed by additional influences and adjustments through the indefinite future.

Impressed with the importance of academic life to the conduct of foreign policy and with the importance of world affairs to higher education, the Carnegie Endowment for International Peace initiated in 1950 an extensive program dealing with universities and world affairs. After an exploratory experience with self-surveys of resources and activities bearing on world affairs, undertaken by nine cooperating colleges and universities, a handbook on *Universities and World Affairs* was published by the

Endowment in 1951 for the use of institutions of higher educa-tion.[1] Pointing out that self-surveys in this field, institution-wide in character, might reveal strengths and weaknesses, duplications or omissions of effort, the handbook suggested that survey-apprais-als could become guides to coordinated effort and the wiser use of available resources, and could provide clues to future lines of development.

The handbook urged American colleges and universities to undertake, at the midpoint of the century, such survey-appraisals as a basis for planning, and it suggested the kinds and scope of self-searching questions appropriate to the scrutiny. Following its publication, the Carnegie Endowment sponsored a series of re-gional conferences to which some three hundred institutions of the United States and Canada sent representatives. At each con-ference the potentialities, the problems, and the techniques of self-surveys were discussed. As a result almost a hundred institu-tions began self-surveys, and by 1956 more than sixty surveys had been completed.

The program of self-surveys was entirely decentralized. The Endowment was not urging upon colleges and universities any specific adjustment or development, but was urging each to con-sider questions and issues of growing importance and complexity. Each cooperating institution appointed a faculty committee, broadly representative of the institution, and this committee planned and carried through the particular kind of inventory and analysis which seemed locally most appropriate and worth while. The Endowment provided a measure of consultative aid and established a central clearinghouse for the exchange of materials and information. The clearinghouse mimeographed institutional survey reports as they were completed and dis-tributed them among the cooperating institutions.

The process of self-survey—that is the self-education of co-operating faculties in respect to the adjustments of their institu-

[1] Howard E. Wilson, *Universities and World Affairs* (New York: Carnegie Endowment for International Peace, 1951).

tions to world conditions—was adequate justification for the general program. The individual surveys were significant as steps in institutional growth. But as the self-survey aspect of the program was completed, it seemed also worth while to synthesize the results of the experience in a series of topical reports. Volumes were planned to deal with international relations in the liberal arts curriculum, the training of specialists in international relations, the function of universities in research about world affairs, the role of colleges and universities in adult education on international matters, the relation of American college life to the world outlook of students, and the handling of foreign students by American universities. Qualified specialists in these fields undertook the preparation of the reports, each drawing fully upon the institutional survey experiences but drawing also upon all other sources of pertinent data. The Endowment completes its program on universities and world affairs by sponsoring publication of these volumes through the American Council on Education.

Throughout the survey experience it became apparent that colleges and universities are increasingly involved in adult education and that international relations are increasingly important in adult education. It was apparent also that few institutions of higher education had thought through their responsibilities and problems in adult education; the need for background analysis and for the development of rational theory is great in university operations in adult education. The present volume in the series of reports growing out of the Endowment program—a volume jointly sponsored by the Endowment and associations in adult education—provides that analysis and rationale. It will be of guiding value, not only to many institutions which have been involved in the survey program, but to all colleges and universities concerned with their role in the education of citizens in world affairs.

HOWARD E. WILSON

September 15, 1956

Contents

FOREWORD vii

EDITOR'S PREFACE xi

1. *Introduction* 1

2. *The Task of the Educator of Adults* 9

3. *Public Opinion and Foreign Affairs* 32

4. *The Distinctive Role of the University
   in World Affairs Education* 45

5. *The Scope of Present Services* 60

6. *Arousing the Interest of the Inattentive Citizen* 79

7. *The Education of the Attentive Citizen* 104

8. *Serving the Actively Concerned* 126

9. *The Further Education of the Specialist* 139

10. *A Positive Program for Action* 145

APPENDIX: SOURCES 167

BIBLIOGRAPHY 170

INDEX 172

CHAPTER ONE

Introduction

THE MATURE American must perform many roles. To conform to the standards he sets for himself and to do what is expected of him by others, he needs to understand and follow a number of distinct, though overlapping, codes of behavior. He directs his own personal growth and advancement. He has specific responsibilities to each of the several members of his family, to his church, to his employer, and to the associations to which he belongs. He has friends who need his help and counsel. He is asked to participate in the political life of his community and sometimes to take his turn as a leader or an office-holder. As a citizen, he must look beyond his own locality to his county, his state, and his country, since he is committed to play a part in shaping the policies of each. Less tangibly but still very clearly he is required to share the burden of world responsibility which his nation has assumed.

The roles themselves are not new, growing, as they do, from basic human conditions and relationships. In every age, some men have had to perform all of these roles, and all men have had to perform some of them. But today they are vastly more complicated than they were in the past. The advance of knowledge has raised the level of understanding required to discharge the responsibilities of each role. To be an adequate parent or citizen or employee or employer requires far more from an individual today than it did fifty years ago. The democratization of political, social, and economic life has required many people to assume obligations which were formerly carried by only a few. The spread of universal suffrage, the growth of voluntary groups, and the diffusion of knowledge through both formal and informal channels constantly extend the area of concern and understanding of an increasing number of persons. Finally, the task of integration, of fitting together the various roles, grows ever more difficult as each role becomes more complex and pervasive. Since the personality is a whole though the roles are many, tension always occurs when one role comes into conflict with another. It is sometimes hard, for example, to be both a responsible citizen and a loving parent— as every mother has learned who has had to send her son away to war.

The American's Newest Role

The newest of the important political roles of the mature American is his obligation to share the burden of his country's participation in world affairs. Forty years ago a sense of responsibility for foreign affairs was felt by only a few. Although Americans have always known a great deal about life in foreign lands because so many were immigrants or the children of immigrants, the new citizens fixed their central attention on the nation they were creating and not on the countries they had left behind. A deep interest in the conduct of foreign relations was usually felt only by a few figures in public life and by those who had sufficient wealth and leisure for education and travel. Today the people of the United States are required to face squarely the fact of their major international position. Every American, unless he willfully averts his eyes, recognizes that he and his country are committed to a continuing relationship with the rest of the world. If he cares about peace, material security, and the life and happiness of his children, he must give thought to the proper nature of this relationship.

In world affairs, as in other concerns of mature men, the conscientious citizen seeks and receives assistance in learning how to act effectively. He has available a greater wealth of information than did any of his ancestors. The knowledge of the specialist and the wisdom of the generalist are provided in profusion. Every day the mass media present vast accumulations of facts and opinions. Thousands of agencies and associations compete for attention. Some of them are openly biased, and others strive for objectivity. The basic institutions of adult education, such as the libraries, the evening schools, and all the various forms of university extension include the understanding of world affairs as one among their many objectives. Anyone who wishes to learn has ample opportunity to do so. His chief problem is likely to be that of selecting what he can use from the great variety of resources available.

Those who provide these resources have their own problems of both ends and means. As the instruments of information and education have grown in size and multiplied in number and diversity, their administrators have found it necessary constantly to reexamine their fundamental premises and processes. What are appropriate goals, and what methods should be used to achieve them? What is actually being accomplished in a field in which measurement of results is usually general and always difficult? What part should education for world affairs play in the total program of agencies that provide general services? These questions are raised more or less specifically and answered more or less rationally by those who administer every agency of organized communication to mature Americans.

The University and World Affairs Education

This book focuses directly on one such agency, the university,[1] in order to consider both the present scope and the appropriate further development of its work in educating adults about world affairs. Institutions of higher learning long ago ceased to be concerned exclusively with cloistered adolescents and accepted the

[1] Many of the observations recorded here apply generally to all institutions of higher learning, and the term "university" is therefore used broadly to refer to all kinds of institutions of collegiate or graduate rank. Where specific reference is made to some single type of institution, such as a liberal arts college or a technical institute, it will be especially identified. Similarly when a comment applies only to a full-fledged university, the context will make that fact clear.

responsibility of providing education for men and women who are actively engaged in fulfilling their many roles in society. The broad scope of the services offered has been described in a number of studies. Never before, however, has the specific goal of adult education for international understanding been singled out for intensive analysis.

This omission is all the more surprising because universities occupy a central place in the teaching of international relations. Since they are the major producers and repositories of learning in our society, they furnish an indispensable foundation of knowledge for intelligent action. Furthermore, in response to demands from without and a sense of obligation within, universities constantly develop and broaden their programs of adult education in world affairs. They also serve as nuclei for widespread community efforts, as originators of pilot programs, and as resources for the work of other organizations and associations.

The president of a state university who examines closely the intricate and varied structure he administers will find that it contains many special programs of world affairs education which reach adults. He may observe, for example, that his institution sponsors: extension classes and correspondence courses in international relations taught by experts; a widespread program of discussion courses led by lay leaders; a series of institutes and conferences in which various citizen groups are brought to the campus for brief, intensive study; a concerted effort by the Cooperative Extension Service to help farm men and women throughout the state understand economic and social conditions in other countries; a program of supervised home and community visitation by foreign scholars resident on the campus; an annual conference of professors and other specialists in international relations; a club service bureau providing program materials and suggestions to voluntary associations throughout the state; radio and television programs broadcast over the university's own stations or made available to commercial channels; a lecture bureau making arrangements for faculty members to speak to the external public; audio-visual production and distribution facilities; specialized bureaus designed for the education of industry or labor; and publications services offering everything from pamphlets to comprehensive research reports. In addition, individual faculty members may independently engage in other kinds of activities: lectures, conferences, committee and organizational work, writing, and other similar methods of communicating ideas to the public and promoting wider understanding.

To follow a single theme in this fashion through all the varied operations of one university is to demonstrate at once the great scope of the services rendered and the impossibility of finding any simple measure of their size or influence. Nor are all kinds of institutions similar. The president of each public or private university, land-grant or liberal arts college, specialized professional or technical school, and junior college would discover that his institution has its own distinctive pattern, shaped by special local conditions and the inventiveness of the faculty in creating or adapting programs of service. Even if it were possible to prepare statistics which accurately describe the situation at any one time, they would be out of date before they could be printed. Many of the existing services were created only recently, and there is no reason to believe that the development of new forms or the growth of old types has ceased. Certainly the directors of present programs are not content with their accomplishments but believe that much still remains to be done, and the presidents and faculties of many colleges and universities are planning to develop or expand their activities.

The study reported in these pages has been based on a determined effort to secure an accurate picture of both past and present practices. This picture has grown out of a close examination of the work of many universities, a more or less cursory glance at the programs of others, two national conferences of university administrators, an analysis of the relevant literature, and many detailed interviews with educational administrators, faculty members, and independent experts.[2] The authors have come to the conclusion, however, that they should use case descriptions only as background and for purposes of illustration. Much of the literature already available in the general field covered by this book is made up of accounts of successful programs, suggestions for specific kinds of activities, and detailed analyses of the work of specific institutions. For those who would like to explore this literature, a bibliography has been prepared.[3] What appears to be needed is not a summary of past or present achievement but an effort to discover the principles that have grown out of that achievement and that will guide future development. The search for these principles is the central aim of this book.

Still another and broader purpose is implicit in these pages. University adult education has many goals; the authors seized only one thread of purpose and followed wherever it led. In the course of their exploration, however, they became aware of the fact that many of the principles and modes of analysis of adult education in world affairs are merely illustrations of far more general processes. Goals are unique to particular fields; but methods of analyzing goals have elements in common, and techniques of successful operation do not vary greatly from one subject to another. The discussion of world affairs education in these pages, therefore, suggests—and is intended to suggest—how those who administer other programs of university adult education may think about and discharge their responsibilities.

The university should discover its function as an educator of adults by examining the roles the mature adult must perform. It fulfills its obligation by helping the adult to carry out his many responsibilities with understanding, satisfaction, and a sense of the relation of these roles to one another.

[2] A detailed report of the method of investigation will be found in the Appendix (pp. 167–69).
[3] See pp. 170–71.

The Content of Subsequent Chapters

While everyone will agree that it is important for citizens to understand world affairs, there is sharp disagreement concerning specific goals and the methods by which such understanding should be brought about. "To understand world affairs" is, in fact, one of those broad objectives which serve, like the stars, to fix a position but offer no other practical help in steering a course from day to day through all kinds of weather. The façade of agreement soon crumbles when the realities of the situation are faced. Certain hard questions must always be answered:

How may the field of world affairs be conceived and defined?

What is the proper role of the citizen in shaping American foreign policy?

How much does the American citizen know about world affairs?

How can education be distinguished from all the other means by which the citizen learns about world affairs?

How can the university identify the groups in the general public to which world affairs education should be directed?

A large body of opinion may be brought to bear on the analysis of these questions from the literature of both international relations and adult education. However, specialists in these two fields have been somewhat confined within the walls of their disciplines and have seldom found it possible to bring their separate sets of conclusions into that degree of interaction which would prove fruitful. The task of chapters 2 and 3 is to sketch, with broad strokes and with no attempt at the portrayal of the nuances known to the close observer, both the range of answers given by various authorities to the questions listed above and the position which appears to the authors to have the greatest validity. Perhaps by this means an introduction may be effected between adult educators and experts in international relations which will lead later to more productive collaboration.

Chapter 4 describes the whole field of adult education in world affairs and suggests the principles which define the distinctive role of the university as it operates within that field.

Chapter 5 presents a general analysis of the kinds of adult educational activities which universities are now sponsoring and deals with the way in which those activities fit within the functions and organizational patterns of institutions of higher learning.

Chapters 6, 7, 8, and 9 make up a single large unit dealing with the kind of education suitable for each of the four major groups of citizens to whom world affairs education should be directed.

Chapter 10 is a general summary and synthesis of the main themes developed in the earlier pages. It offers a program of action based upon a review of the ends desired, the means available, the distinctive role of the university, and the ways of overcoming the deterrents which now stand in the way of a comprehensive development of education in world affairs.

CHAPTER TWO

The Task of the Educator of Adults

THE CONVICTION that every citizen should know all he can about world affairs is so widely urged from every rostrum and in every medium of print that it appears to be a universal belief of the leaders of society. Discussions about international relations are not otherwise noted for either consistency or unanimity of viewpoint, but the prescription of education is suggested by all diagnosticians of the present world scene, some of them sternly, some of them wryly, most of them hopefully.

The chain of reasoning which is used to demonstrate the need for education is sometimes elaborated at great length, but it can, in essence, be reduced to a straightforward series of propositions:

1. Democracy is the best form of government.
2. In a democracy, decisions about policy are ultimately made by the people.
3. The quality of these decisions depends upon the degree of enlightenment of the people.
4. The increase of enlightenment can only be achieved by education.
5. Among the decisions which must be made in every democracy are those which have to do with foreign affairs.
6. Therefore, education in foreign affairs is essential for the wise conduct of foreign affairs in a democracy.

Thus, nakedly stated, runs the argument. To these propositions, three more are often added:

7. At present, the most crucial public issues are those related to foreign affairs.

8. The average citizen knows far less about foreign affairs than about domestic issues.

9. Therefore, the most crucial public task for education today is to create a better understanding of foreign affairs.

Since most men do not act as though these assertions are self-evident, elaborate demonstrations of their truth are often considered necessary, and, when positive argument fails, the consequences of a lack of education are graphically portrayed, most often by the picture of a mushroom cloud rising above a devastated city.

Who Learns about World Affairs—and How?

Those who advance the argument outlined above are usually well aware of the degree of ignorance which prevails about world affairs. What general observation suggests about this ignorance, research confirms. Those who analyze the level of American knowledge and opinion by scientific sampling procedures have discovered in many studies how little is known and understood about international relations by the people as a whole.[1] A few facts from one such study suggest the usual findings. In the spring of 1953, a survey of a representative sample of Americans made by the International Press Institute showed that 26 percent of the people were unable to name any of the countries fighting on our side in Korea and only 56 percent could identify the major point which caused the truce talks in Korea to bog down for so long. Only 21 percent knew the meaning of the letters "NATO," and even fewer (16 percent) knew what the organization is and does.[2]

If the American people know so few facts, one can only be

---

[1] Similar studies often reveal a shocking ignorance about domestic public issues as well—but that is not the subject with which the authors are here concerned.

[2] International Press Institute, *The Flow of the News* (Zurich: International Press Institute, 1953), pp. 229, 232.

pessimistic about what they understand. In an analysis of such studies, Martin Kriesberg came to the conclusion that:

About 30 percent of the electorate, on the average, is *unaware* of almost any given event in American foreign affairs.

About 45 percent of the electorate is *aware* of important events in the field but cannot be considered *informed*. These people retain little information. Although they may follow discussions of the issues of foreign policy, they cannot frame intelligent arguments about them.

Only 25 percent of the electorate consistently shows knowledge of foreign problems.[3]

The reasons for this general lack of knowledge and understanding are not hard to find. Perhaps the average European does not know any more about international relations than the average American,[4] but certainly life in the United States is not as conducive to a knowledge of foreign affairs as is life in Europe. The American nation has only recently taken up its responsible position on the world scene, whereas every European has felt from birth the direct and constant impact of his country's relationships with its neighbors. The geographic isolation of the United States, its great size, its relatively self-sufficient economy, its single dominant language, its basic similarity of cultural patterns, and its merciful escape from the direct experience of war or enemy occupation have caused its citizens to be more shielded from a knowledge of the outside world than are those who live in Europe.

In the United States, direct firsthand knowledge of foreign countries has, in the past, been possessed by either the upper or the lower class, chiefly the latter. Persons with wealth go to foreign schools, travel for pleasure, and often have investments or business contacts which take them abroad. They form a highly visible and influential top stratum of American life. The roots of many other Americans are not deeply embedded in the soil of this

[3] Kriesberg, "Dark Areas of Ignorance," in Lester Markel and others, *Public Opinion and Foreign Policy* (New York: Published for the Council on Foreign Relations by Harper & Bros., 1949), p. 51.

[4] The authors could find no data which would provide a valid comparison.

country. The 1950 census showed that 7 percent were foreign born and another 16 percent had one or more foreign parents. These new Americans do not exert a political influence commensurate with their numbers, but their strength is increasing, particularly as they achieve greater sophistication and economic success. The interest in foreign affairs expressed by Italian-Americans, Polish-Americans, German-Americans, and other nationality groups is perhaps more specific than that evidenced by those who have had the opportunity for foreign education and travel, but interest in the country of origin often runs deep, as every president and secretary of state can testify.

Many of the migrants to this country, however, came with the firm intention of turning their backs upon the places of their origin and tried to become full-fledged American citizens as quickly as possible. Their isolationism has been not ignorance or apathy but positive repudiation. As quickly as possible, they have tried to identify themselves with the 77 percent of the population who have no first- or second-generation ties abroad.

Where does that large proportion of the population learn about foreign affairs? Perhaps the greatest single influence has been the fighting of foreign wars, which has sent so many overseas and given them and their families and friends a keen awareness of other parts of the world. In addition, civilian governmental service, private business, pleasure, and study are taking increasing numbers abroad each year, although it is only recently, with the development of rapid and cheap transportation and the astonishing rise in the standard of living, that the middle class has been able to become familiar at firsthand with life abroad. In spite of these influences, the great majority of the people have never been outside the United States. For them the stimulus to learn about foreign affairs comes from the information presented through the mass media of communication, from the special-interest groups to which they belong, and from other purposeful or casual associations.

During the past thirty-five years, there has been a great increase in the amount of information about world affairs that has been spread by the mass media. The two basic causes for this spread are doubtless the greater involvement of the United States Government in international relationships and the rapid rise of the educational level of the public. In 1920 the American gained his knowledge of foreign affairs from newspapers and a few weekly or monthly periodicals. The only news magazine with a wide circulation, the *Literary Digest,* was chiefly made up of excerpts and digests of opinion drawn from the daily press. In the years since then, the amount of foreign coverage has greatly increased, the circulation of newspapers has risen, and at least three news magazines with large national circulations have replaced the *Literary Digest.* Newsreels and documentary motion pictures have played an increasingly important part. Even more significant, because of the size of their audiences and the directness and immediacy of their impact, have been the two newer media, radio and television.

The effect of these sources of information has been heightened by other purposeful efforts to inform the American public about foreign affairs. The supply of information from the State Department has greatly increased, and public relations experts operating from countless other bases have sought to influence and broaden the flow of the news. Specialized world affairs groups have tried to spread greater understanding of world affairs and foreign policy. The exchange of visitors among nations has been fostered so that direct firsthand contact might promote enlightenment on both sides. All kinds of voluntary associations of lay citizens have been encouraged to adopt special programs designed to inform their members about foreign affairs. Other efforts are legion, and their influence is great.

Since schools and universities are the most prominent agencies of formal education in American life, it is natural that most of the sustained efforts to enlighten the public about world affairs have hitherto been directed toward the children and young people who make up their typical student bodies. The other volumes in this series portray the many and varied approaches to more effective understanding which are now being made on the campuses of American universities. Elementary and secondary schools have also been imaginative in trying to give their students a broader understanding of other cultures and an awareness of the nature and complexity of world problems.[5]

These efforts to broaden formal schooling in childhood and youth have not yet reached a majority of the people. The average American adult has less than a tenth-grade education, and most people who are now mature attended school before the beginning of the modern emphasis on international understanding. Even today, many young people do not complete the secondary school, and only about one-third of them go on to the university. Furthermore, most of the students at both levels probably do not make any systematic study of world affairs. The situation is constantly improving, but still only a small percentage of those who come to maturity have been given any clear conception of the state system, power politics, sovereignty, the influence of geography and natural resources upon national policies and aspirations, the operation of population pressures, the influence of race and religion, the economic interdependence of nations, the history and nature of diplomacy and of formal international agreements, and the record of this country in dealing with other powers.

The effort to provide young people with a basic grounding in international relations should certainly continue so far as it can be carried out within an over-all framework of sound general and professional education. For three important reasons, how-

[5] See, for example:

a) Committee on International Relations of the National Education Association, the Association for Supervision and Curriculum Development, and the National Council for the Social Studies, *Education for International Understanding in American Schools* (Washington: National Education Association, 1948).

b) Educational Policies Commission, *American Education and International Tensions* (Washington: Educational Policies Commission of the National Education Association and the American Association of School Administrators, 1949).

ever, the education of adults in this field is at least as important as the education of young people. First, full comprehension of international relations requires an adult mind and adult experience; those who study the subject in youth can lay only a groundwork for more precise and discerning study later on. Second, the problems of foreign affairs are urgent and require immediate attention; they will not conveniently wait for the next generation to solve them. Finally, and most fundamentally, the next generation will be no better prepared than this one unless the mature citizens, who so greatly influence the curriculum of the schools and colleges, become convinced by their own experience that an understanding of foreign affairs is an essential element in the education of all young people.

The Approach to the Subject
of International Relations

What should be learned by one who aims at the comprehension of world affairs? Both the citizen himself and the educator of adults [6] are likely, when asked that question, to assume at first that an answer can be found simply by turning to the international relations experts. Surely there must be some basic stock of ideas, some coherent discipline whose central emphases are clear and whose boundaries are fairly well marked. But the conscientious person who tries to gain a general comprehension of the field of international relations soon discovers that while, in some respects, it appears to be a unified discipline, in other respects it is a collection of different, though related, disciplines. For some special-

---

[6] The term "educator of adults" is used throughout this book to refer collectively to all individuals and groups who plan and direct educational programs for mature people. Some educators of adults have such duties as their sole or major assignment. These include the heads and staff members of university extension divisions, Cooperative Extension Services, evening schools, and world affairs councils. Often, however, the responsibility for adult education is only a part-time activity of such people as professors of international relations, the staff members of area studies institutes, librarians, or the executives of various special-interest groups.

ists the focus is upon international politics; for others, international law; for others, diplomacy; for still others, international organization or world trade.[7] Among all these, it is hard to discover any core of knowledge or any central group of issues. While this lack of integration is not unique to the subject of international relations, the emphases and the focuses of attention in other fields, such as physics, botany, geology, psychology, and economics, seem more sharply defined.

The specialists in international relations who are members of university faculties have been particularly concerned with the problem of definition because they must fit their own field of study into the comprehensive curriculums of their institutions. When international relations was first proposed as a new discipline within the social sciences, the proposal was opposed by some who held that no such separate field existed. The basic areas of knowledge already had been charted, and each of them had its international aspects. To cut away segments of political science, economics, history, sociology, and anthropology, it was said, would only rob those disciplines and produce no new synthesis with a sound theoretical base. International organization, for example, rests in part on principles of political theory, which are taught in the political science department. How can the study of national and supranational forms of government be sharply separated? The student of one must be a student of the other. If a new department of international relations were to be created, one of two undesirable consequences would result. Either the subject matter would have to be divided, bringing about a lack of integration, or two departments would have to offer the same courses, producing needless duplication. This is only one example of many. Speaking more generally, it was argued by the opponents of the proposed field that the subjects taught by a professor of international relations have their natural home in one of the basic disciplines, that all data in the social sciences are relevant to inter-

[7] See another volume to be published in this series, Dale Fuller, *Training of Specialists in International Relations.*

national relations, and that knowledge should not be further fragmented.

The issue is not restricted to American universities. Indeed, the problem may be felt more sharply in Europe than in the United States. A gathering in England of professors of international relations from nine countries gloomily contemplated a paper which listed contemporary doubts about their field under the following headings: "As to its very existence," "As to its nature," "As to its social value," "As to its unitary character," "As to its necessity," "As to its academic merits," "As to its technical feasibility," and "As to staffing possibilities." The last-mentioned point was subdivided into three questions: "What can one do?" "Where shall the needed wisdom be found?" "Whom could we trust?"[8] Although the gathering was made up of those who might be thought to be particularly sympathetic to the new subject, there were marked differences in the defining of approaches to it. The conference found that it could agree only that "the study of International Relations has among the social sciences a place the importance of which has not yet received due recognition."[9]

Despite the obstacles put in their way, the proponents of international relations as a separate field have established their position on many university campuses. In the past twenty years, there has been a steady growth of courses, departments, institutes, and committees. While the definition of content varies from person to person, all who regard international relations as a separate discipline maintain that the body of knowledge which deals with the relations of peoples and countries with one another is different in nature from knowledge of other aspects of social life. An inter-

[8] Geoffrey L. Goodwin (ed.), *The University Teaching of International Relations*, International Studies Conference (Oxford: B. H. Blackwell, Ltd., 1951), pp. 14–22. The paper cited was prepared by Professor C. A. W. Manning of the University of London. The entire report is an excellent illustration of the issues involved in this controversy as well as of the operations of the professorial mind.

[9] *Ibid.*, p. 36.

national organization, for example, resembles a national government only superficially and analogically. The absence of sovereignty, the need to work collectively, the relative weakness of the means of enforcing decisions, the complex problems of representation of nations, and the great diversity of interests and attitudes are but a few of the special factors which distinguish an international body from others. Comparisons of the operations of international law and politics with national law and politics will call attention to marked differences despite certain common elements. Furthermore, some basic areas of subject matter, as, for example, the subject of war, appear to be more appropriate for study by a specialist in international relations than by anyone else.

The proponents of this point of view are fond of pointing out that any fair analysis of the social sciences would assign to the study of international relations its own territory and status, complete with all the perquisites of sovereignty, including the right to make treaties with other disciplines; that any other conclusion is merely the defense of boundaries set up long ago in the infancy of objective social inquiry; and that these boundaries, like many others, should long since have been renegotiated.

In the past ten years, however, there has been a growing conviction of the unsoundness of the argument that any social fact can be clearly identified as the primary property of a single discipline. The walls which formerly established the boundaries are crumbling as emphasis is placed more and more upon the idea of a discipline as a mode of analysis rather than as a division of the terrain. Kirk has made this point very well:

> Today, distinctions among the older divisions of the social studies are, in many cases, due less to separateness in subject-matter than to the fact that each is engaged in examining the same set of phenomena from a slightly different point of view. The sociologist, the historian, the political scientist—all are required to be synthesizers to some degree.[10]

[10] Grayson Kirk, *The Study of International Relations in American Colleges and Universities* (New York: Council on Foreign Relations, 1947), pp. 11–12.

With this change in the fundamental conception of the social sciences, the older controversy about the place of the study of international relations became relatively meaningless. Each discipline is a way of analyzing a body of data; it is expected that some of the same data will be useful in different ways to other disciplines. This second position, by its promise of freedom rather than restriction, has been increasingly accepted until it is now dominant in defining the field.

Thus, international relations is seen in the universities as an inquiry made by many men of diverse backgrounds but with a common focus. Every approach to the content of international relations is colored by the background and convictions of the person making the observation. Each man begins his analysis of the world, its divisions, and the relationships of those divisions to one another by a reference to his own area of expertness and his central convictions. The geographer, the anthropologist, the student of law, the political scientist, the economist, the historian, the linguist, and the sociologist—all approach their tasks differently. So, too, do those who have special interests in the solution of specific problems: the churchman, the educator, the expert in public health, the proponent of political reform, the agriculturist, the industrialist, and the dietitian. Even within the broad boundaries of each major field, a wide variation of interpretation exists.

Yet it is not surprising that specialists in international relations, while developing an increasing awareness of the value of many approaches, also see the need for unity and synthesis. The tendency of every disciplined mind is toward an economy of assumptions, and simplicity and consistency of interpretation. There is a body of facts and events—mainly, though not exclusively, made up of the relations among nations—which constitutes the material for the discipline. The object of the discipline is to explain these facts and events by the exposition of true, meaningful, and useful generalizations. Special insights into certain of these facts and events will come from the international lawyer, others from the diplomatic historian, and still others from the economist. But the task of international relations as a whole is to bring together, organize, and unify the parts.

Thus, international relations is now being seen by its most comprehensive students as a discipline of *synthesis,* bringing together all those fields of study which contribute either directly or indirectly to an understanding of the relations among states, governments, and peoples.[11] But if it is true that this synthesis is the object of the discipline, then a discipline of international relations has not yet been formulated.[12] What now exist are partial formulations of the whole or well-developed formulations of some of the parts—for example, international law and military science.

The development of this synthesis will doubtless provide a set of basic propositions of great value to the citizen and the educator of adults. By its very nature, this synthesis will consist of the most basic and fundamental elements, taking what is essential from each of the parts. It will not of itself answer all the questions involved in citizen education, since that will not be its primary function. But it will illuminate and clarify the whole field and will, therefore, provide a necessary focus for all efforts to educate.

The citizen (and those who are concerned with his education in world affairs) will reach the end of this brief description of the academic field of international relations with certain conclusions.

First, each citizen, like each specialist,[13] approaches the study of world affairs from a special vantage point which is all his own. An interest in learning more about international relations is usually rooted in some immediate personal concern. To the businessman and the farmer, the possibility of selling commodities

[11] The fullest development of this viewpoint is found in Quincy Wright, *The Study of International Relations* (New York: Appleton-Century-Crofts, Inc., 1955). See especially chaps. i–v.

[12] *Ibid.,* p. 501.

[13] The specialist is, of course, a citizen himself and is so dealt with in later pages. The proper terms at this point might be "specialist citizen" and "nonspecialist citizen," but they are so awkward that the simpler, though less exact, expressions are used here.

abroad provides an opportunity, and the competition of foreign goods presents a threat. To those who furnish leadership in voluntary associations—unions, churches, fraternal orders, service organizations, or groups of citizens seeking special reforms—the contact with parallel leaders or associations abroad offers both a stimulation and a challenge. Professional workers are interested in their colleagues in other countries. Personal contacts with foreign visitors, recreational travel abroad, attendance at a lecture or film showing, the desire to share the interest of a friend, an interest in missionary work in a church, membership in a group which has foreign affairs as one of its concerns—these and many other associations and events provide the starting point for an interest in international relations. Most important of all is the hope for peace and the feeling of responsible citizens that peace might be achieved if they could know more about international relations than they do.

Second, the citizen will recognize that it is pointless merely to wander through the vast terrain of international relations in search of some central highroad. The best he can hope for at this time is a map. Such maps are to be found in rich abundance and all of them are useful, but each of them has been made by a man or a group of men chiefly interested in specific features of the landscape. The boundaries of the discipline of international relations are not so clearly defined as are those of geometry or English grammar or organic chemistry.

As this discipline develops and takes shape in future years, it will have increasingly distinctive values for both the specialist and the citizen. The specialist will find that his specialty, whether it be international law or military science or diplomacy, is illuminated by a synthesizing view. He will receive a broader understanding of the whole and will discover elements which make him a better specialist as well. The citizen, too, will find that a synthesis will not only give him a comprehensive understanding of the field, but also illuminate the particular concern which initially aroused his interest in world affairs.

Third, the present aim of the citizen must be to create his own synthesis. He has become interested in the subject for any one of a number of reasons, he usually has a very particular goal in mind, and he brings to his study the whole mass of his previous learnings and beliefs. His awareness and concern with foreign affairs will rest finally on the insights he achieves from his own distinctive approach to the field. The wise man will not seek formulas by which to measure and judge the new facts he encounters; he will instead seek an understanding which is based on an integrated structure of knowledge and value but which is constantly growing and broadening as new evidence is brought to bear on what he has previously learned. The key concept is that put forward by Professor Manning, when he said that the purpose of university courses in the field is:

> . . . to meet the needs of a student who wants to achieve a progressively deeper insight into the nature of international relationships—the relations, that is, between peoples and states—and an ever improving aptitude for appreciating an international situation as it presents itself to the experienced statesman's eye. The purpose, in a word, is to support the student's efforts towards an understanding of life—as life goes on in the society of states.[14]

Direct and Indirect Learning

The educator of adults has the task of helping citizens build a bridge between their specific interests and a more general understanding of international relations. The means he uses to achieve this end are usually determined by his conception of the nature of the educational process.

Since all experience of every sort leaves some effect on the individual, it is often argued or assumed that experience and education are the same thing. It is common for those who adopt this large conception to talk of the educative effect of better housing, slum clearance, commercial mass media, and all the other aspects of modern life. *The Education of Henry Adams*

[14] Goodwin (ed.), *op. cit.*, p. 14.

did not describe merely the formal schooling and other purposeful learning of the young Brahmin from Boston. It dealt with
the influence on him of his whole environment and the cumulative
consequences of all his acts. This position is an ancient one. Plato
said that the statesman should establish those laws which would
lead the citizen into the path of virtue. The general task of education in every age, according to this view, is to reconstruct the
environment or the processes of living to condition the citizen in
desirable ways. In the field of world affairs, those who use this
approach lay great emphasis upon travel, better news coverage,
building an acquaintance with people of other countries and cultures, and all the other means of enriching normal human experiences so that they have a maximum impact.

To equate experience and education, however, is to ignore the
fact that some kinds of experience are undertaken with a deliberate effort to learn and, therefore, differ in both their nature and
their effect from casual or random activities undertaken as a
matter of habit or in pursuit of other ends. One who says, "I
want to learn more about world affairs," and proceeds methodi-
cally to do so is far more likely to have a full and rounded view
of the subject than one who is merely following an impulse, a
habit, or a desire to be amused. A week in a foreign country is
more instructive to one who tries to examine and study its cus-
toms and institutions than to one who goes there for the same
amount of time only because it happens to be a scheduled stop on
a vacation tour. As Roger Ascham pointed out four hundred
years ago: "Learning teacheth more in one year than experience
in twenty." The wish to learn is never constant but varies in its
intensity from casual and vague inclinations to sharp, clear, and
focused desires. Other things being equal, the educative effect of
any experience varies with the intensity of the purpose.

There appears to be a valid distinction, therefore, between
direct learning, which results from those activities undertaken
with at least some intent to be educated, and indirect learning,
which is a concomitant of all the experiences of life. Even those

activities undertaken for specific educational purposes may produce learning which was not intended; one who attends a lecture seeking only a few facts is often led, by the personality or approach of the speaker, to gain insights or opinions which are entirely unexpected.

Direct learning has a deep influence, but, since most of life is carried on without a conscious desire for improvement, the sheer quantity of indirect learning is very great. Many persons seldom or never embark on sustained efforts to improve themselves and can be reached only by some reshaping of the environment in which they lead their ordinary lives. Furthermore, many ideas, particularly unfamiliar and upsetting ideas, can be made palatable only if they are presented by indirection. George Bernard Shaw wrote both plays and prefaces, but his plays had by far the greater impact. His audiences came to be amused; they left, laughing at his audacity but thinking about what his characters had said.

Mass Campaigns

During the past fifty years, what growth there has been in international understanding on the part of the American people has been largely brought about by indirect learning, resulting from such basic factors as the improvement of transportation and communication, the rise of menacing foreign powers in Europe and Asia, and the invention of new weapons of destruction. Because of the impact of this indirect learning, many of those who are concerned with adult education for world affairs have tended to ignore the difference between direct and indirect learning or to believe that the former is of comparatively minor significance. These educators of adults carry out their programs of citizen education through the mass media or by other similar efforts to take information to large numbers of people on the assumption that if knowledge is available, it will be absorbed.

The commercial mass media—television, radio, motion pictures, newspapers, magazines, and books—provide most of the sources of information to the citizen. He turns to them to be entertained and to keep informed about at least some of the aspects of modern life. Those who control the mass media have a great opportunity, therefore, to use their powerful contacts with the citizen to broaden his understanding. Furthermore, those who espouse special causes, of which an understanding of world affairs is only one, tend to think, because of the demonstrated appeal of mass media to the public, that they are the major avenue to the mind of the citizen. These media also provide an example for other mass approaches, such as lectures, exhibits, and special films and publications.

Faith in the power of mass campaigns has also been supported by other arguments or assumptions. Because of the critical need for world understanding, there has naturally been a desire to have educational programs produce widespread and rapid results. The success of commercial advertising has given the practice of organized public relations a position of respect in our society. The students of public opinion have demonstrated clearly and on a broad scale that mass campaigns produce specific results. As a result, many people have assumed that deeper kinds of learning may be achieved in the same way. Most important of all, perhaps, is the fact that the institutions and programs of sustained adult education are only now growing into a sufficient strength, prominence, and flexibility to provide the means for direct learning experiences. It was necessary for society to depend heavily on the provision of opportunities for indirect learning until more immediate, purposeful, and inventive means could be developed and made widely available.

But the data presented earlier in this chapter clearly show that the majority of the American people do not yet possess an adequate knowledge and understanding of world affairs. Nor does the building of still more intensified and extended informational programs offer much hope. Such, at any rate, is the conclusion which may be drawn from two studies made in Cincinnati by the National Opinion Research Center. In September 1947 interviews were held with a scientifically determined sample of the residents of that city in order to discover their knowledge about, and attitudes toward, the United Nations.[15] There then ensued an imaginative and highly intensified campaign to provide more information on this subject by the use of all the mass media and through several of the largest citizen organizations.

In March 1948 a second series of interviews was held.[16] The results showed that the campaign had had no discernible effect in widening the interest of the people in world affairs, in giving them more information, or in changing their general orientation. In the opinion of those who conducted this experiment, it proved:

> . . . that the creating of interest is the first measure in building public opinion and that only after that will information be absorbed. The effort in any educational enterprise is very great in comparison with its immediate effects, as this campaign shows. Therefore, the more that is found out about the learning process and the teaching function on a mass scale, the more may that labor be reduced.[17]

It is not hard to understand why mass campaigns have such limitations as educational devices. The common elements of all mass approaches are these: they are directed not to a specific, clearly known and identified group but to a general and undifferentiated audience; they do not permit any coherent and integrated response on the part of those to whom communication is directed; and they are essentially discontinuous in that each individual item of communication must stand by itself, carrying its particular message without being part of an ordered series of experiences for the reader, viewer, or listener. In other words, mass approaches inherently lack three of the basic elements which are required to effect substantial changes in the people

[15] National Opinion Research Center, "Cincinnati Looks at the United Nations," Report No. 37 (Mimeographed; Chicago: The Center, University of Chicago [n.d.]).

[16] National Opinion Research Center, "Cincinnati Looks Again," Report No. 37A (Mimeographed; Chicago: The Center, University of Chicago [n.d.]).

[17] Shirley A. Star and Helen MacGill Hughes, "Report on an Educational Campaign: The Cincinnati Plan for the United Nations," *American Journal of Sociology*, LV (1950), 400.

reached: an intimate knowledge of the particular nature and needs of the learner, a method whereby the learner may actively respond and participate in the learning process, and an integrated and planned-for cumulative effect.

These shortcomings can be alleviated in some measure. A newspaper, for example, can departmentalize its various sections to aim at certain broad groups in the population; it can encourage readers to write to the editor; it can build continuity by employing a group of feature writers and columnists who have their own following; and it can be sure that each story which presents a new set of facts also gives a brief background and interpretation. The use of these and other devices, however, merely illustrates the attempts of the newspaper to overcome its basic weaknesses as an instrument of education.

The process of indirect learning through mass approaches works—but it works at a low level. The reader, viewer, or listener gradually absorbs many facts, but only rarely is he helped to organize them into an integrated point of view. He unconsciously accepts certain values, but he does not hold them deeply because he has never examined them. He adopts various generalizations which he does not understand and cannot fit together coherently. He does not even long remember the facts, values, or explanations because he has not really learned them very deeply. The result in the area of international relations has been graphically described by Walter Lippmann:

> There is no mystery about why there is such a tendency for popular opinion to be wrong in judging war and peace. Strategic and diplomatic decisions call for a kind of knowledge—not to speak of an experience and a seasoned judgment—which cannot be had by glancing at newspapers, listening to snatches of radio comment, watching politicians perform on television, hearing occasional lectures, and reading a few books. It would not be enough to make a man competent to decide whether to amputate a leg, and it is not enough to qualify him to choose war or peace, to arm or not to arm, to intervene or to withdraw, to fight on or to negotiate.[18]

18 Lippmann, *Essays in the Public Philosophy* (Boston: Little, Brown & Co., 1955), pp. 24–25.

Direct and Specialized Approaches

It is because inadequacy is so inevitably a result of an exclusive reliance on indirect learning that greater attention is being given to the development of direct learning experiences as a means of educating the adult public. "When a man's knowledge is not in order, the more of it he has the greater will be his confusion," said Herbert Spencer, and all those who have become disillusioned with mass campaigns will heartily agree. In world affairs education, the great failure of such campaigns is that they do not provide people with a framework of basic ideas about international relations around which to build a further knowledge.

The educator of adults in this field always has two central tasks: to arouse an initial interest in world affairs in men and women not yet aware of its significance to them; and to provide opportunities for interested citizens to broaden their knowledge and deepen their insight. As we have seen earlier, world affairs is a field of study which is approached by many avenues, and those who have an actual or potential concern with international relations come from highly diverse backgrounds. Therefore, in pursuing either of the two central tasks, the educator of adults who wishes to develop direct learning experiences cannot merely prescribe a set course or series of lectures and insist that all men and women should attend it.

His responsibility is to determine the specific audience he hopes to serve, to analyze its nature and desires, and to design the kinds of educative experiences it needs, defining specific objectives and selecting the content and methods by which those objectives may be attained most effectively. In planning his program, he is able to use the three principles which are inherently difficult in mass campaigns. He can, for example, provide for continued learning, which is essential to the growth of understanding. He can also devise ways by which learners share in all stages of the educative process, thus providing both the heightened interest which results from cooperative planning and the mastery which comes only when there is an opportunity to ask questions, to call for the illustration of principles, to discuss, or otherwise to gain the values which arise from active participation rather than passive reception.

This kind of approach is slow and often laborious. It seldom offers any prospect of immediately spectacular results or of widespread acclaim. Each program begins by reaching only a relatively small number of people, and later growth is often only gradual. These natural consequences of direct learning often appear to be serious limitations to those who are impatient for quick results. In view of the results of the Cincinnati study, however, it may be doubted that any quicker results are possible. Apparently, an integrated and sustained view of world affairs demands the use of direct and specialized programs rather than mass campaigns.

However, the direct and indirect approaches to learning should not be viewed as competitors but as complementary to each other. In the long run, only the use of both means of learning can produce a citizenry capable of intelligent interpretation, shaping, and support of foreign policy. Mass campaigns can rapidly and efficiently convey a specific set of facts to large numbers of the people. Moreover, these campaigns often create a spark of interest which leads to participation in a program of direct learning; now that such programs are becoming widespread, this possibility is constantly increasing. More significant, perhaps, is the fact that mass campaigns and the mass media generally provide one important means of continuing education for those who have already achieved a basic conception of the field of world affairs.

Consider, for example, how most people read the newspaper. Each person who does so tends more or less unconsciously to select for close reading those items which have some meaning or interest for him. What he remembers is, at least in part, a product of the intensity of his interest and the purpose which leads him to read particular items. Suppose that a foreign correspondent covering an Italian election tries to dramatize it by showing how the campaign is going in Milan. A reader leafing through the pages of the newspaper finds his attention caught because his family came originally from Milan. He reads the story quickly to see if there is any mention of the places or people he has heard described. Having skimmed the article, he turns the page. In his mind linger bits of fact and adopted attitudes which go to join the others he has absorbed in the past; but a week later he will have forgotten the facts and may have to be reminded that he has ever read the article at all. A much clearer picture will be carried away by a person who reads the same story because he is aware of the importance of the election campaign as a part of the international battle between democracy and communism. His reading will be closer; he will evaluate the facts more intently; and he will have a more accurate framework into which to fit the new facts and interpretations.

The great advantage which arises from the attempt to build a sound central synthesis through direct learning is that it provides the base for the constant enlargement of understanding. The study of international relations is, in some senses, a lifelong series of case studies. If one is searching for the principles which lie behind the cases, each new situation as it arises can be seen in perspective and evaluated. There is, as well, an inner structure to support the accumulation of more knowledge. The continuous stream of facts brought by random experience does not merely flow by but is integrated with the facts already possessed. When a man's knowledge is in order, the more of it he has, the greater will be his enlightenment.

Conclusion

The gloomy words of Walter Lippmann quoted earlier in this chapter suggest that popular judgment cannot be considered a sound basis for the determination of the crucial issues involving war and peace. This conclusion might well lead those who feel the need for a sound American foreign policy to argue that citizens should be kept from exercising any control over issues concerned with international relations. If this course of action were to be followed, the educator of adults would have no responsibilities in the field of world affairs. Few people would seriously suggest, however, that power should or can be removed from the citizen. They might well argue as to *how* his responsibilities should be exercised, and chapter 3 points out some of the complexities of this question. But the issue as to *whether* the citizen should exercise power was settled long ago—and unmistakably in the affirmative. Since citizens have the power to shape foreign policy, they must be helped to exercise it intelligently and to base their decisions on an understanding of the issues involved. The responsibility of the educator of adults must be conceived in the broadest terms. Whatever his specific goal, his general aim must be to make democratic decisions wiser.

CHAPTER THREE

Public Opinion and Foreign Affairs

THE EXCELLENCE of our constitution consists in the balance of three powers," observed Horace Walpole. "Unfortunately it is the nature of a balance to fluctuate by a breath of air." That breath of air, which sometimes attains hurricane force, is ordinarily called public opinion, and its influence is keenly felt by both political theorists and practical politicians in every society where governmental decisions are determined by the will of the people. No realist could deny the influence of popular opinion on every public issue at every level of American government. Those who occupy both legislative seats and senior executive posts achieve their positions by the votes of their fellow men, and Mr. Dooley has suggested that even the Supreme Court follows the elections.

But as the suffrage has been extended and as the population has grown, government has become more remote and more complex; far greater reliance has had to be placed on those who have the specialized skills required to administer the massive machinery of the body politic. A road or a dam can be built only by an engineer, a civil service system can be administered only by an expert in personnel, and a school system requires the supervision of a qualified educational administrator. And yet all these people owe a responsibility to the citizens for whose benefit the work of government is performed. A balance must constantly be struck between expert public service and ultimate public control. This balance is as necessary in foreign affairs as in domestic policy. The appropriate role of public opinion in the conduct of foreign policy must be discovered so that it may serve as a guide in developing educational programs which will equip the citizenry to exercise properly its ultimate control.

Before discussing specific educational programs, the composition of the various groups which make up "the public" should be indicated. Such an analysis will serve to forewarn the unwary educator who tries to plan a single world affairs program to suit everyone. There are, in reality, many publics, and it will become apparent that they differ in such significant ways as will suggest special opportunities, as well as obstacles, to the educator of adults in dealing with each of them.

A Description of the Public

"Public opinion" generally implies a rather mystical composite of the varied views of all segments of the population. In fact, each such segment has certain identifiable general predispositions and specific views which have been distilled from a combination of facts and misinformation, of altruism and special interest, of understanding and prejudice. Those who believe in education expect that their efforts will create a more intelligent, sensitive, and responsible public opinion by building within each of the publics a sound basis of understanding and by stimulating the will to use that understanding in the public interest as well as for individual advancement.

Those who provide education must take into account the staggering diversities in age, education, background, income level, places of residence, and occupation of the people. Anybody who contends that any single plan of education is capable of reaching all the people or even a majority of them is naïve. Each program turns out eventually to have its own natural audience, and those who announce that they intend to "educate the American people" by some single plan are often astonished to discover how narrow a segment of the population they finally reach. Countless forums on world affairs have been organized for "the whole community," but the sponsorship and the particular characteristics of the program have inevitably attracted, in each case, only a certain portion of the citizenry. Unless a plan of education begins by defining—and defining sharply—its target audience, it runs the danger of dissipating its efforts. Knowing precisely for whom the program is intended provides an essential guide to both content and method.

For the purpose of planning a program of education in international relations, the most useful analysis of the adult population divides citizens into groups according to their knowledge and concern about world affairs. If all citizens are placed in a continuum on this basis, four broad divisions can be marked out. Each of these can be described briefly here; more detailed descriptions will be appropriate later.[1]

At the lower end of the scale is the large bulk of the public—inattentive, uninformed. This group has little or no conception of international relations as a separate field of interest or inquiry. This inert sector is so preponderant that it colors with its own hue any picture of the general public which emerges from public opinion polls. The characteristics of ignorance and unconcern, which have been described and documented in the previous chapter, are the distinguishing marks of the man who falls within this first division—the inattentive citizen.

At the next level is the attentive citizen.[2] He is informed and interested. He may not have extensive knowledge, and his interest in world affairs may be no greater than his interest in a host of other public questions. But he has some understanding of the importance of foreign policy, and he follows with some perception the major debates on these issues as they confront the nation. He reads at least a few of the popular magazines and belongs to at least one organization which occasionally offers a program concerned with some public question.

[1] See chaps. 6–9.
[2] This term is used by Gabriel A. Almond in his excellent study, *The American People and Foreign Policy* (New York: Harcourt, Brace & Co., 1950). Professor Almond, however, also includes within this term those who are here called the "actively concerned."

The actively concerned citizen, next in the continuum, has a special interest in world affairs. He seeks opportunities to learn more about international relations and regards the field as a major avocational interest. He may also be the advocate of a special solution to the problems of war and peace. Often he has an interest in a certain area of the world or in some special aspect of world affairs—international economics, underdeveloped areas, politics, or American foreign policy. Ordinarily he feels not only a personal concern but, in addition, a desire to persuade others of the importance of world affairs. He gets pleasure and satisfaction from the active pursuit of this interest. His enthusiasm may occasionally overtake his good judgment. He is likely to belong to several civic organizations and to be a leader in at least one.

Finally, there is the specialist. He is a citizen too, but for him, unlike the others described above, international relations, or some aspect of the field, is his occupation. This is his central concern. Typically he has received special training, and he usually has, in addition, firsthand experience of world affairs from on-the-spot observation. He may be a professor of international law in a university or a civil servant in the Department of State, an economic adviser to a large international business corporation, or a member of the staff of a United Nations commission. He is a professional. His competence may lie in his ability to perform services or in his comprehensive knowledge; usually he has some of both.

This fourfold classification helps define the general tasks of adult education in world affairs. The average citizen is the inattentive one: the task here is to find ways of engaging his attention, for direct attempts at education without first creating interest will surely fail. The aim then is simply to move him into the next class; he needs to become an attentive citizen. The attentive citizen, in turn, can be assisted in his effort to gain more knowledge and understanding so that he can better interpret world events as they unfold; as a result, he may also become more active in his concern. The actively concerned citizen needs to be given the opportunity to broaden and deepen his knowledge; he can also be helped to act more skillfully in his attempts to engage the interest of other citizens. The specialists need opportunities to educate one another both within the confines of their particular specialities and across these boundaries.

Educators of adults will recognize at once that the division of the public into these four groups does not require the rigid separation of each group into a segregated program. A single learning activity may be planned for several groups, but it will not be successful unless each of them is kept clearly in mind. Distinctions are useful even when at their extremes they flow into one another. The separation of powers in the American federal system is a crucial distinction of functions, though it turns out that each of the three branches occasionally exercises authority more akin to another's than to its own. Similarly the classification of the publics will help the educator to construct and differentiate his activities, though on occasion there will be a desirable intermingling of these groups.

The Public and Representative Government

Representative democracy places the ultimate determination of policies in the hands of the public. This proposition of itself, however, does not state what are in fact the different roles of the four distinct publics in the democratic process, nor does it indicate what relationship exists or ought to exist between the representative and the represented. The answers to both of these questions will prove of importance to the subject of this book because they help to indicate the *kind* and the *degree* of knowledge required by each public in order to assure the successful operation of representative government.

Since the great bulk of the public is generally inattentive and unconcerned, only grave crises produce any response at all. A sudden awareness may develop as a tense situation in Europe or Asia threatens an outbreak of war, but the character of the public's response is determined by deeply ingrained traits and habits. There is no immediate development of a rational analysis of alternatives; "the reaction is still a mood, a superficial and fluctuating response."[3] And such unstable reactions from the inattentive public will strongly influence the tone of foreign policies so long as the attentive public, together with the actively concerned and the specialists, remain a small (even though influential) minority. The responses of the latter take the form of a more rational consideration of alternatives. An attempt is made to understand, even to formulate, a policy which takes into account not only what is desirable but also what is possible— facts as well as wishes.

Given the superficial and fluctuating response of a generally inattentive public, and the schematic division of the public into its vast inattentive and its much smaller attentive, actively concerned, and specialist components, what conclusions may be drawn concerning the role of these publics in the formulation of policy?

First, official government policies should not emerge as direct, immediate, and unassessed reflections of public sentiment. Sound policy and today's opinion poll are not identical. A mass cannot govern, says Walter Lippmann;[4] it is a premise of representative government that the prevailing public sentiment is only one of many factors that must be taken into account in determining what the public interest requires. Edmund Burke's statement to the electors of Bristol provides an appraisal of the representative's duty as appropriate for Americans now as it was for his British audience in 1774:

Your representative owes you, not his industry only, but his judgment; and he betrays, instead of serving you, if he sacrifices it to your opinion. . . .

To deliver an opinion is the right of all men; that of constituents is a weighty and respectable opinion, which a representative ought always

[3] Almond, *ibid.*, p. 53.
[4] Lippmann, *Essays in the Public Philosophy* (Boston: Little, Brown & Co., 1955), p. 20.

to rejoice to hear, and which he ought always most seriously to consider. But *authoritative* instructions, *mandates* issued, which a member is bound blindly and implicitly to obey, to vote, and to argue for, though contrary to the clearest conviction of his judgment and conscience; these are things utterly unknown to the laws of this land, and which arise from a fundamental mistake of the whole order and tenor of our constitution.[5]

Second, public officials in executive posts must accept responsibility for invention, formulation, and assessment of policies in the public interest, so that well-considered alternatives are open to the choice of the governed. The public may not always make its final determination intelligently, but its choices are much more likely to be fatal or crippling if the responsible leaders offer policies based on popularity and momentary sentiment rather than upon the hard realities confronting the nation. Hamilton argued in defense of this principle as follows:

When occasions present themselves, in which the interests of the people are at variance with their inclinations, it is the duty of the persons whom they have appointed to be the guardians of those interests, to withstand the temporary delusion, in order to give them time and opportunity for more cool and sedate reflection.[6]

Third, legislative representatives must be urged to act not merely as mirrors of the immediate and transient interests of their constituents; they must be expected to express as best they can the public interest. But since the public interest is "what men would choose if they saw clearly, thought rationally, acted distinterestedly and benevolently,"[7] and since the public as a whole, because of the preponderance of its inattentive base, rarely does any of these things, we shall also expect a canny weighing by

[5] Edmund Burke, in a statement to the electors of Bristol, November 3, 1774, from Ross J. S. Hoffman and Paul Levack (ed.), *Burke's Politics: Selected Writings and Speeches of Edmund Burke on Reform, Revolution, and War* (New York: Alfred A. Knopf, 1949), pp. 115–16.

[6] Alexander Hamilton, in *The Federalist* (New York: The Modern Library, 1941), Number 71, p. 465.

[7] Lippmann, *op. cit.*, p. 42.

the legislator of what is required against what is desired, since his excellence depends upon the former and his re-election upon the latter.

Fourth, the inattentive public cannot be expected to respond to policy questions with thoughtful consideration of the complicated alternatives, for here mood governs. This mood, in turn, sets the limits within which the government can act. These limits may seriously impair the society in crises, either by refusing the government those powers which it needs to meet the crisis, or by endangering the freedom of the society by granting authority beyond what the situation requires. Two things need to be done to mitigate these ill effects. One is to attempt to modify public attitudes; the other is to attempt constantly to persuade as many as possible of this vast body to become a part of the attentive public. Increasing the size of the attentive public and correspondingly reducing the size of the inattentive public should result in a significant improvement in the quality of public response. Chapter 6 will suggest some of the ways by which these results might be brought about.

Fifth, the attentive public and the actively concerned can be expected to weigh with some wisdom the broad questions of public policy which confront the nation. A discussion of these groups, of what their members need to know in order to weigh these questions, and of the university's responsibility to them is the function of chapters 7 and 8.

Sixth, the specialists, in and out of government, can be expected to interpret, criticize, formulate, and invent policies with vigor and with a high regard for what they conceive to be the public interest. While major responsibility is placed on our elected officials for policy formation, the specialists provide a strong mediating influence by which policies are criticized and interpreted for the benefit of both the officials and the attentive public. Chapter 9 discusses the ways in which the university can serve the needs of the specialists.

Public Opinion on Foreign Policy

All the above considerations, however, appear to apply to the role of public opinion in domestic as much as in foreign affairs. What are the special factors which affect the influence of public opinion on the conduct of foreign policy? Since the end of the Second World War a number of thoughtful writers have considered this question.[8] The problem is not a new one (it has received the attention of Thomas Jefferson, Alexander Hamilton, Alexis de Tocqueville, James Bryce, and Woodrow Wilson, among others), but modern conditions have highlighted its significance.

In the first place, the very nature of foreign policy calls for relations between the government and the public that are sharply different from those involved in domestic affairs. There is no over-all arena of decision which permits the conflicting vital interests of nations to be defined and compromised by public debate and majority vote. Domestic questions are resolved within the framework of law and government, but in the relations between nations there is no overarching government. Although there is a large body of international law, it does not usually extend to the most vital interests of the parties involved, for the nations have chosen to defend these by sovereign power. Each nation has worked out ways by which its foreign affairs can be conducted to meet the needs of this situation. The constitutional provisions governing the conduct of foreign relations in the United States, the remoteness of private interests, the occasional

[8] See especially:

a) Walter Lippmann, *op. cit.*

b) George F. Kennan, *Realities of American Foreign Policy*, The Stafford Little Lectures at Princeton University, 1954 (Princeton, N. J.: Princeton University Press, 1954), especially chap. 4.

c) Hans J. Morgenthau, "Conduct of American Foreign Policy," in Hans J. Morgenthau and Kenneth W. Thompson (eds.), *Principles and Problems of International Politics* (New York: Alfred A. Knopf, 1950), pp. 163–73.

d) Mulford Q. Sibley, in a Symposium, "Can Foreign Policy Be Democratic?" *American Perspective*, II (1948), 155–62.

e) Thomas A. Bailey, "The Dilemma of Democracy," *American Perspective*, II (1948), 211–17.

necessity for secrecy, and the modern conditions of warfare are all factors which distinguish the conduct of foreign relations from the conduct of domestic affairs. Each of these factors is briefly reviewed below.

The President's initiative in treaty-making, his position as Commander-in-Chief of the Army and the Navy, his power of appointment of our diplomatic representatives, and his reception of diplomatic representatives of foreign powers are prescribed by the Constitution. These have led some to the conclusion which Jefferson reached that "the transaction of business with foreign nations is executive altogether." Justice Sutherland in the Curtiss-Wright case speaks of "the very delicate, plenary and exclusive power of the President as the sole organ of the federal government in the field of international relations."[9] But since the legislative branch has the power to declare war, to pass upon treaties, to raise the armies which the President commands, and to grant or withhold funds, there is in practice a divided control, though the initiative may remain exclusively executive. The important fact for our consideration here is that, while in domestic matters the legislator acts on behalf of his constituents in the enactment of laws which are initiated and adopted in the legislative branch, the legislator's scope of action and opportunity with respect to foreign affairs is much more sharply limited by constitutional provisions. Thus, the image of the public speaking through its representatives with the many voices of its varied interests and desires concerning domestic matters is replaced in part by the image of the President speaking with one voice—the united voice of the whole nation—in foreign affairs.

Second, the effect of foreign policies on the interests of the individual citizen is much less readily understood than is the case with most domestic policies. In the progression of constantly larger orbits of influence, ranging from local community affairs to the grand strategy of world politics, the sense of reality steadily diminishes. The citizen may be intimately concerned with the life

[9] *United States* v. *Curtiss-Wright Export Corp., et al.* (299 U.S. 304) 1936.

of his own community, but, as he reflects upon foreign affairs, he is less able to discern his own interests. It is persuasively argued in the defense of democratic government that no one can tell as well as the people themselves "where the shoe pinches" and what services the government should provide, but in the case of foreign policy the very complexity of the issues makes it difficult to pass such a judgment,[10] for in foreign affairs the well-being and safety of the nation as a whole must be considered irrespective of particular individual or sectional interests.

Third, the conduct of foreign affairs occasionally requires a degree of secrecy which inevitably affects the citizen's, and even his representative's, capacity to pass judgment. Diplomacy requires negotiation, and successful negotiation requires the making of the kind of concession which is virtually impossible in public. To lay bare the whole record subsequently might, as George Washington claimed, "have a pernicious influence on future negotiations, or produce immediate inconveniences, perhaps danger and mischief, in relation to other powers."[11] Furthermore, secrecy concerning vital military information is essential to the safety of the nation in times of peril; there is no way of informing the American people without informing the whole world. Even if only that minimum of secrecy is permitted which is necessary for the successful conduct of delicate negotiations and for keeping vital military data from enemies or potential enemies, situations will arise in which the capacity of the citizen to pass judgment will be impaired by an unavoidable ignorance on relevant matters. While this is an almost intolerable condition when it extends to domestic policy, it is one of the necessary, if occasional, consequences of foreign involvement.

Finally, modern conditions of warfare can create crises in which defensive action is required—if any defense is to be made— before it is possible to obtain the judgment of the people and

[10] Cf. James Bryce, *Modern Democracies* (2 vols.; New York: Macmillan Co., 1921), II, 367–83.
[11] Quoted in *United States* v. *Curtiss-Wright Export Corp., et al.,* (299 U.S. 304) 1936.

even, on occasion, of their representatives. Thomas Bailey has asked his readers to suppose a situation in which unimpeachable sources advise the President that an enemy is planning to dispatch forty-eight hours hence a fleet of bombers capable of destroying major cities and killing thirty million people.[12] In such a case there is little doubt of what the public would expect of the President, but it is equally clear that, if Congress were not in session, there would be little opportunity for the public to express its views even through its representatives. Other cases require more difficult, though less consequential, decisions. President Truman's action in committing forces in the Korean War is a case in point; the delay which would have resulted from a full debate on the merits of the case would almost surely have meant the loss of the peninsula to the enemy. The speed with which decisive military force can be brought to bear in modern warfare thus offers an additional obstacle to the impingement of public opinion on foreign policy.

These factors suggest that there exists a tension between two conflicting principles. On the one hand, the conditions within which foreign policy must operate require a certain latitude of action on the part of the executive in the pursuit of the public interest. On the other hand, the problems themselves are of such grave import that their solution deserves the careful guidance of an informed public. The tension between these apparently opposite requirements helps to define the task of adult education in world affairs. Can a program of education be devised which realistically meets both these necessities? What are the kinds of questions which require wide public debate and what kinds are to be left within the discretionary power of the executive? What are the ways in which an educated public can give sound guidance to the direction of foreign policy while recognizing the limitations on the deliberative processes within which modern democracies must operate? There is an urgent necessity for a sharp definition of the kinds of knowledge which the attentive

[12] Bailey, *op. cit.*

public, the actively concerned, and the specialist need to possess so that executive discretion and ultimate public control can fulfill their appropriate functions in the conduct of a successful and democratic foreign policy.

Each of these three publics, and the inattentive public as well, is the subject of separate consideration in chapters 6–9. The scope of this volume, however, is further defined by its limitation to the university's role in the education of the citizen. The next two chapters attempt to define that role and to describe the scope of present services.

CHAPTER FOUR

The Distinctive Role of the University in World Affairs Education

THE PURSUIT of learning is a basic human process occurring throughout life and exhibiting itself in countless ways. Usually it is a private act or series of acts arising out of a sense of need or interest and is wholly contained within the consciousness of the individual. Even the child learns far more outside school than he ever does inside it. The adult, since he is usually not compelled by law or social custom to attend any formal institution of learning, is even more responsible than the child for continuing his own education.

In every civilized society, however, there are programs and institutions which provide more or less formal means by which adults may learn together. A historian of American culture, for example, can trace countless institutions which offered instruction or provided the framework for collaborative study. In colonial days, the church usually assumed this function. Even before the nation was founded, however, there had come into existence the philosophical societies, the Juntos, and the proprietary schools which were the precursors of the far more extensive movements of the nineteenth century: the lyceums, the evening schools, the reading circles, the summer camp meetings, the chautauquas, and the extension lectures. In the twentieth century, the number, variety, and size of these programs increased very rapidly; it is now estimated that almost fifty million adults participate annually in some form of sequential learning activity.[1] This figure, which is

[1] Malcolm S. Knowles, "Adult Education in the United States," *Adult Education*, V (1955), 76.

derived by adding together the actual or estimated enrollments of various institutions, probably does not make due allowance for duplications, for optimistic guesses, or for activities which can be called "educational" only by a generous use of that term. Even if the estimate were reduced by as much as 50 percent, however, the number of adults pursuing education would still be far larger than is generally realized.

The desire to learn about world affairs is usually satisfied by individualized learning rather than by participation in an organized program. Probably only a small part of the fifty million enrollments mentioned above was motivated by an interest in international relations. Even that small part, however, is spread through many different kinds of institutions and associations. It is impossible either to understand the organized world affairs education of the present or to estimate its potential growth in the future without being aware of the broad range and scope of adult education.

The work of each agency is conditioned by the part which it plays in the whole field. When the university is seen as but one of many adult educational institutions, its distinctive role in world affairs education becomes much clearer.

Organization of Adult Education

Organized adult education can best be defined, not by establishing its boundaries, which are almost impossible to trace, but by locating its centers of purpose and influence. Each of the other levels of education has its major institutional form. Secondary education, for example, is centrally concerned with the work of the high school, although there are many other programs designed to teach adolescents. But no single major institution dominates the field of adult education. Instead, there is a complex of agencies, wholly or partially devoted to adult education, with a seemingly endless variety of purposes and programs. The life of children is built around the expectation that they will go to school, and the types of institutions which instruct them are relatively few in number, although each is of great size. Adults ordinarily must fit their education into other more basic concerns, and therefore the scope and range of the programs which provide adult education are as complex as the total pattern of mature life. These programs are too numerous to be counted and too varied to be sorted into clear-cut categories.

Adult education agencies do, however, fall into certain natural groupings, differentiated on the basis of major similarities of purpose and operation.

BASIC FRAMEWORK

The first distinction has to do with basic framework. Some agencies are primarily built around an ordered structure of authority; these are here called "organizations." Others, here called "associations," are built around the principle of voluntary membership. In the Middle Ages, a university might follow one or the other of these two basic patterns. The University of Paris was an organization of teachers who attracted students, while the University of Bologna was an association of students who engaged teachers. Today, the university is invariably an organization, as are many of the other basic agencies which provide adult education: the public school, the museum, the settlement house, the community center, and the industrial firm which has its own training program. There are, however, many agencies whose educational programs are carried out for their voluntary memberships: men's service clubs, unions, women's groups, and the whole range of associations which exist to achieve special purposes for their members or for society.

The operating differences between organizations and associations run very deep. The way in which purposes are clarified, the nature of the program of education itself, the relationship of that program to the over-all structure, and the method of appraising success or failure are all affected. The dean of an evening college and the executive of a local world affairs council may both want to educate their local publics about international relations, but they will go about that task in different ways.

CENTRALIZATION OF PURPOSE

The second distinction is between those programs that focus all their activities on a specific purpose and those programs that direct their efforts toward the accomplishment of a number of purposes. The first group of organizations and associations have a direct approach, they have limited the boundaries of their interest, and often they achieve an intense concentration in their work. Examples of this type in the field of world affairs education are the Carnegie Endowment for International Peace, the Council on Foreign Relations, the Foreign Policy Association, the American-Scandinavian Foundation, Freedom House, the United World Federalists, and the English-Speaking Union. The second group of programs have a more general responsibility and attempt to achieve a number of different goals, striking some kind of balance among them. Examples of the second group are evening schools, community councils, chambers of commerce, cooperatives, and generalized fairs and expositions.

RELATION OF EDUCATION TO PRIMARY PURPOSE

There is yet another way in which purpose divides adult education programs into groups, this time in a three-part classification.

Some programs have education as a primary purpose. The Cooperative Extension Service, for example, attempts to improve performance in farming and homemaking entirely through instructional means. Direct service to the farmer and the homemaker and the administration of regulatory controls have sometimes in the past been a part of the task of the county agents, but neither is accepted as a basic function today. Similarly, in the other instructional programs of the universities, the public schools, and many proprietary or endowed institutions, the focus is entirely on teaching and learning; other purposes, if any, are subsidiary. In the institutions which educate both young people and adults, some problems often exist as to how much of the resources should be devoted to each group, but the central intent to educate is a matter of unanimous agreement.

In other programs, education is a function coordinate with other functions. A museum must preserve knowledge and undertake research as well as educate, and so, too, must the university viewed as a whole. A public library must consider education, recreation, information-giving, research, and aesthetic appreciation to be parallel purposes. An association is often as much interested in building the fraternal spirit of its members or in pursuing a legislative or promotional campaign as it is in education. In each such case, a special problem of definition and clarification exists. There is an enormous literature, for example, dealing with the way in which the public library should define its adult educational role and distinguish it from other basic purposes.

Still a third group of programs is built around the idea that education is only a subordinate or facilitating function. Perhaps more programs fall within this category than in either of the other two. An industrial firm usually provides education for its employees because it wishes to improve their performance in their jobs. A union establishes an educational program for its members because it hopes to weld the membership into a stronger and more cohesive unit. A church uses education as one means to help people find salvation. Government departments of health, welfare, traffic safety, conservation, defense, and correction use education as a way of achieving their substantive purposes. In all such cases, the test of success is whether the program of instruction has achieved the goal which was set for it. The basic question is not whether an individual or a group has learned something but whether that learning contributes to the achievement of the broader goal for which the program was established.

As the distinctions of purpose and structure operate together, they create the groupings of basic types of programs to which reference was made earlier. Table 1 presents a schematic outline which identifies and illustrates these fundamental forms.

Further kinds of analysis are possible in an almost endless variation. One might, for example, distinguish between public and

TABLE 1

VARIOUS TYPES OF ADULT EDUCATIONAL PROGRAMS

STRUCTURE AND FUNCTION	TYPICAL PROGRAMS	
	Directed Specifically to World Affairs Education	Directed Toward a Number of Goals Including World Affairs Education
Organizations considering education to be a primary function	(I) American Foundation for Political Education	(II) Evening colleges
Associations considering education to be a primary function	(III) World affairs councils	(IV) League of Women Voters
Organizations considering education to be a function coordinate with various other functions	(V) Specialized library on international relations	(VI) Public libraries
Associations considering education to be a function coordinate with various other functions	(VII) American Association for the United Nations	(VIII) Junior Chamber of Commerce
Organizations considering education to be only a subordinate or facilitating function	(IX) Program established by an industry to train its overseas personnel	(X) Program established by an industry to provide generalized educational opportunities for all its personnel
Associations considering education to be only a subordinate or facilitating function	(XI) Group of union leaders studying world trade in order to work out union policy	(XII) Program established by a union to provide generalized educational opportunities for all its members

private institutions or between national and local programs, or use as criteria such factors as method, age of persons served, or historical background. Eventually, of course, one would end with the infinite and subtle distinctions which give each program its own identity. If all these other distinctions are examined closely, however, it will usually be found that the three identified in the foregoing analysis and in the chart are the most fundamental and basic in establishing the inherent structure of the whole field of adult education.

One important qualification must be made. The category of specialized agencies has here been illustrated by using those which are concerned with world affairs education. There are many other specialized categories, dealing, for example, with health, consumer understanding, improved family living, safety, and all those other fields in which men have decided that particular goals should be the focus of their educational efforts. The methods used by specialized agencies in world affairs education and by other specialized agencies have a great deal in common. The director of a world affairs council and the head of a local association for family living, for example, can engage in a great deal of useful discussion about such matters as organization, money-raising, instructional techniques, and methods of evaluation.

Since the pattern of agencies and programs providing adult education is extraordinarily complicated, it is necessary to examine rigorously any generalization that purports to cover the whole field. In the process of exploration and development of the last twenty-five years, there has been a tendency to announce that some principle which has an undoubted value in a segment of the field is universal in its application. To some people, the community is all-important; to others, the group or the individual takes a central place. A new technique of teaching, a new device for locating needs and interests, or a new method of evaluation is often put forward as the answer to the problems of every program. As each claim of this sort is made, it is salutary to examine the variety of situations summarized in Table 1 and consider how many of them would find the new proposal useful.

The educator of adults in any one program may, however, find it profitable to know the ways in which his work parallels that undertaken in other similar programs. Such agencies as evening colleges, evening high schools, proprietary and endowed schools, and residential short-course centers all fall in Type II (as defined in Table 1), and the staffs of these various agencies will find that they can readily undertake, and profit from, a common consideration of their problems. Workers in each of the other types will also find a great similarity in their interests and problems.

It is as useful to recognize points of difference as of similarity. As each person defines the bases on which his work differs from that of others in the field, he usually finds that the areas of agreement and possible collaboration become much clearer. The dean of an evening college must be primarily concerned with the education of his students in terms of their own needs and interests. The director of an industrial training program, on the other hand, must think of the education he sponsors as an instrument to accomplish other purposes. The two can often work out jointly sponsored programs—but not unless each understands and respects the other's position.

There is a marked tendency for the programs which lie on either side of one of the central points of distinction suggested above to move toward the other side. An association, as it grows, engages a staff of workers, and soon a hierarchy of authority begins to appear. An organization often extends the base of its support by building subsidiary associations, as when a university fosters the growth of an alumni group. A specialized agency broadens its work to include a number of goals, and a generalized agency often concentrates an increasing part of its resources on accomplishment of a single objective. A program which is purely educational when it begins may, in the course of time, take on coordinate functions or even develop goals which appear to be more important than the education provided. Thus, an evening college may begin for purely educational reasons, gradually take on recreational or community-improvement functions, and wind up as a means by which money is raised for the parent institution. A similar shift can occur in the reverse direction. Because of such changes, programs usually do not remain completely consistent in adhering rigidly to the basic types suggested in the table. A shift and flow is constantly taking place. Yet as a program moves, it moves toward another type, and the categorization of the basic clusters therefore shows both the present status of a program and the main directions of its possible future change.

Guiding Principles for the University

A university, being a large and complex institution, may undertake programs of adult education which fall into any one of the twelve basic types. The extension division may include world affairs as part of its broad program for the community (Type II in Table 1), or it may have a special unit designed specifically to provide education in international relations (I). Its alumni association may sponsor general (IV) or specific programs (III). The university may maintain a special institute which combines research and teaching either in world affairs (V) or in adult education generally (VI), or it may provide housing and some supervision for the offices of an association organized on either basis (VII, VIII). The university may enter into a contract with an outside organization or association which wishes to provide either specific or generalized training for its staff or members (IX, X, XI, XII). The university president mentioned in chapter 1, who is amazed to discover all of the kinds of work his institution is undertaking, will also be surprised to find how the various programs sort themselves out among the basic categories.

There is in fact so much to do and so many ways to do it that few would wish to say that a university should never embark on any type of activity to which it might be invited or drawn.

Since resources are always limited, however, the university educator of adults is constantly being faced with problems of choice. Usually these problems are of two sorts. The first occurs when the educator is presented with a number of attractive possibilities, of which only one or a limited number can be chosen. The second occurs when he wishes to undertake some new activity and must select the plan which has the greatest promise of success.

As experience with adult education has lengthened, certain principles have gradually emerged to define the proper role of the university in this field. These principles are not accepted universally as dogma, but, in the ceaseless discussion of ends and means in which university educators of adults engage, certain basic ideas have clearly become the professed or hidden determinants for the choice of activities or the guides for future action.

EDUCATION THE PRIMARY PURPOSE OF THE UNIVERSITY

First, the university has an obligation to consider education as a primary purpose. This principle implies that those who provide instruction must constantly focus their attention on the basic needs and interests of the students themselves. The university should not embark on an adult educational program because it wishes to build public relations, gain profits, or support the other parts of its work. These happy consequences may indeed result, but usually not if they are directly sought, for adults are even shrewder than their children in recognizing and resenting materialistic motives. The university teaches undergraduates or medical students, not because it wants to make money or build its popularity, but because it believes that such teaching serves a vital social purpose. It should be equally zealous in safeguarding its integrity in teaching its mature students.

Since world affairs education is concerned with an area of unusual tension today, the university should be particularly careful to retain its central focus on educational purposes lest it slip gradually into the serving of other purposes and thereby eventually lose its basic freedom to choose what it shall do. The difficulty arises everywhere, but it is particularly evident when the university accepts a contract for educational service or engages in a collaborative program. The case is clear enough so far as extreme positions are concerned. No American university would take on the responsibility for deliberately indoctrinating a group of students in a special social theory, such as communism or fascism, nor would it consciously embark on a program in which only one side of a basic issue, such as the tariff question or American immigration policy, could be presented.

The university has a fundamental obligation to attempt to give its students a balanced and impartial view. The principle that education should be the primary purpose of the university is not easy, or simple, to follow. Its application must be made by men of intelligence and discrimination, and even they will often find specific decisions difficult to make. But unless they have the principle, they will have no basis at all for their decisions.

EMPHASIS ON THE USE OF HIGHER MENTAL POWERS

Second, the university should emphasize educational activities which call for the use of the higher powers of the mind. The purpose of the university today, as always, is to provide advanced learning, and it should not change its goal when it turns to the education of a new group of students. As one university president discussing this question put it, the only appropriate activities are "those which a college can give with respect and with its faculty maintaining dignity." There are many other associations and institutions which have the responsibility to develop simpler forms of instruction, and the university should not relieve them of their duty by invading their proper areas of work. This test, like the previous one, must be applied subjectively, and it is to be expected that honorable men will occasionally disagree. Nonetheless, the test should be made.

This principle is often misunderstood to mean that the university should provide for adults exactly the same courses of study it provides for young people on the campus. Only in this way, it is said, can standards be maintained. In reality, the reverse is true, for one who uses this argument is departing from standards traditionally upheld by the university. The course on the campus was planned with the needs of the students in mind and was built carefully into a sequence of study. To wrest the course from its context and offer it unchanged to an entirely different group of students is to do violence to the basic idea of education. The campus course may indeed be a useful point of departure as a tested and selected body of content. As we have seen in chapter 2, however, the field of international relations is far from being rigidly defined. In that field, therefore, it is particularly necessary to rethink any "regular" course for use with adults to be certain that the needs and interests of mature people will be served and that the program offered fits the university's broad purposes in educating citizens concerning world affairs.

PIONEERING IN WORLD AFFAIRS EDUCATION

Third, the university should be a pioneer in developing new forms of education. In the great expansion of adult education which is now taking place, one of the chief requisites is inventiveness in building new activities. The university is in an unusually good position to take the leadership in creating new educational ideas because it possesses such great resources of leadership. Its faculties have both knowledge and an understanding of how to convey it. A pioneering spirit in world affairs education is particularly necessary because the university campus contains such a large percentage of the experts in international relations. No other adult educational agency has so clear a mandate for leadership.

In working out this third principle, the university may occasionally appear to violate the rule that it should restrict its offering to higher intellectual activities. For example, a university may agree to collaborate with a labor union in the development of a special course designed for the members of that union who may have had little previous knowledge of, or experience with, world affairs. Under such circumstances, it would be folly to insist that the rigors of usual university work should be applied. The course, if it is to be developed for a large general audience, must be pitched at a level that permits the communication of general (although crucial) concepts. Some would argue, therefore, that the course should not be given by the university at all.

But the university, in entering such an agreement, is not seeking a new group of students for itself. It is, instead, using its talents and resources to meet a social need. The processes of constructing objectives, selecting content and methods, evaluating, trying and retrying the course, and gradually bringing it into acceptable form require skills of a very high order, and it is entirely appropriate for university faculty members to devote their time to them. When these difficult tasks have been completed, it is time enough for the university to withdraw and let the union expand the program by itself.

Each professor who teaches adults must be to some extent a pioneer. Sometimes men whose lives have been lived in academic communities hardly know how to behave when they are faced with the task of stimulating truly mature minds. On the campus, they may have come to rely on the customary sanctions—such as compulsory attendance, and the awarding of grades, credits, and degrees—which surround college teaching but which apply in adult education only if the adults concerned are willing to put themselves into the instructional patterns of youth. Most adults are not inclined to do so. The professor who goes out into the community to teach must, therefore, face the challenge of the new audience and see how he can interest, stimulate, and teach the mature minds which await him. It is a matter of common observation that the professors who are the outstanding teachers on the campus are the most successful teachers of adults, precisely because they have never depended on the sanctions and routines which support their less able colleagues.

COLLABORATION WITH OTHER COMMUNITY AGENCIES

Fourth, the university should collaborate with the many other agencies in society which educate adults. In the higher education of young people the university and the college have a virtual monopoly; in the field of adult education, they do not. Unaware of the new situation, the university is often tempted to pay little attention to the work of the other agencies or even to enter into competition with them. While both of these courses of action are occasionally necessary, it is usually wise to lay primary emphasis on finding the ways in which collaborative working relationships may be established. The university has limited resources with which to work, and it is well to husband them by influencing other agencies to undertake duties which otherwise the university would have to perform. Also, collaboration usually means that the university can influence, and help to guide, the work of other agencies while itself reaping many benefits so far as community relationships are concerned. Sometimes the educator of adults is afraid he will lower the status of the university if he works with other agencies, but this result does not follow if the educator himself has standards to which he firmly adheres. By working with other agencies, the university may, in fact, heighten the general understanding of its appropriate role and responsibilities.

EDUCATION OF LEADERS

Fifth and finally, the university should give special consideration to the education of leaders. This principle has long been inherent in the very idea of the university itself, and it is particularly appropriate so far as adult education is concerned. When the university says, as it has traditionally said, that it is training young people to be leaders for society, its critics sometimes imply that it is acting as an instrument of snobbish discrimination, as it did in England in the eighteenth century, when, as Charles C. Gillispie has commented, "The only important thing . . . coming out of the English universities was the English governing class."[2] When the university educates adults, however, it is not serving as a primary leader-selecting mechanism. It is dealing with people who have already established their positions or are in the process of doing so.

The task of adult education is so great that it must enlist the services of many kinds of agencies. If the university attempts to educate everyone, it will usually build a rather undistinguished record. Even worse, standards will have to be lowered to such an extent that the leaders of society will not have the stimulus to education which the university is so eminently able to give them. "Leaders" in this sense does not imply any one elite based on money or tradition or power. It refers to those individuals who provide guidance and direction for others at every level of society and in every sphere of activity. In government, in business, in voluntary associations, in unions, in the professions, and in all other formal and informal social groupings, some individuals emerge with positions of responsibility and authority. If the university can reach and help these persons, it will greatly heighten the effect of the education which it provides. And unless the university does reach them, they may not be reached by any other form of organized adult education.

These five principles may be used by other agencies than the university, but, taken all together, they suggest its central function. By concentrating its energies in the directions suggested, it can offer a well-defined program of education to the adult, and give strength, focus, and leadership to all other efforts in the community to provide a balanced program of world affairs education.

[2] Gillispie, "English Ideas of the University in the Nineteenth Century," in *The Modern University*, ed. Margaret Clapp (Ithaca, N. Y.: Cornell University Press, 1950), p. 27.

CHAPTER FIVE

The Scope of Present Services

A MERICAN UNIVERSITIES have developed many kinds of adult educational activity, and all of them have been used to build a better understanding of world affairs. In this chapter an attempt will be made to show the variety of approaches now being employed and to consider how these new adult educational services influence the function and the structure of the university.

No listing of activities could leave out of account the manifold undertakings of individual faculty members acting on their own initiative. They write, give lectures, participate in panels and discussions, and express their views in other ways. They organize citizen groups and serve as influential leaders within them. They sponsor and publicize special events. They introduce foreign visitors to American homes and audiences. They work in other formal and informal ways to spread an understanding of international affairs among their fellow citizens. Their activities are, in fact, so numerous and varied as to defy complete classification.

This volume, however, is concerned primarily with the programs which are officially sponsored by universities, and, while these programs are remarkably varied, they do have basic similarities. Adult educational activities usually appear at the growing edges of universities as they interact with the outside community. A person or a group on the staff of a university identifies a need for service and creates a program which is especially designed to meet that need, and which, to some extent, is unique. But similar institutions tend to have similar patterns of growth, and at university after university, programs of service are being created afresh, with no realization that the same problem is being solved in much the same fashion elsewhere. When a program becomes notably successful, however, other universities are stimulated to follow the example set for them. The net result of both invention and imitation is that, while university adult education has so great a spread that its boundaries cannot be sharply defined, a common core of programs is very widely found.

The diversity of origin of these activities means that they do not fit together into any single logical classification. Some of the services are developed originally on the basis of *content.* The staff of a professional school, for example, may see the need for the extension of its own area of subject matter and organize a bureau for that purpose or assign to some of its faculty the special responsibility of working with adults. Other services are established primarily to meet the needs of a particular group of *persons to be served.* The Cooperative Extension Service, with its broad program of assistance to farmers and homemakers, is the outstanding illustration of programs of this type. Still other services are organized in terms of the *method used.* Extension-class programs, lecture bureaus, centers to distribute audio-visual aids, and correspondence divisions use their distinctive processes to define their operational patterns. Finally, some services are built up around *physical facilities.* This type is illustrated by the programs developed in connection with a building to house short courses, a radio station, an extension center in the heart of a city, or a university press.

The Programs Most Frequently Found

The following list of the major kinds of university adult education describes actual programs as they have come into being. It is not an idealization or an attempt to impose consistency where consistency does not exist. The list suggests the range of services available and shows, by a few examples in each case, the way in which imaginative educators of adults have used it for world affairs education.

1. *Regular university courses originally developed for young people but scheduled at times or places convenient for adults.* These courses are offered on the campus itself, at organized extension centers, or on a geographically decentralized basis with classes held in various kinds of physical facilities.

Formal courses in international relations, foreign trade, or area studies are frequently offered in extension course programs. They are taken by people who are fulfilling degree requirements, who have specific (usually occupational) interests in world affairs, or who have a general concern with the subject and use this means of finding out more about it.

2. *Lengthy course sequences designed especially for adults.* Sometimes these are the usual degree patterns made up of customary courses. Sometimes they combine such courses in new ways and lead to special certificates. Sometimes they represent completely fresh approaches, with courses being developed and combined in terms of the distinctive needs of adults. Course sequences may be offered on the campus itself or in extension centers or, less often, in a decentralized fashion.

In many such course sequences, some attention is given to world affairs education as a required or an elective topic. In a number of cases, special certificate programs have been constructed, usually around vocational interests, and world affairs is sometimes included as an essential part of the study. World economic problems, for example, may figure prominently in a course sequence for business executives. There is also a growing tendency for evening colleges to develop new programs of general education which, because they are often based on an analysis of contemporary problems rather than the traditional curriculum, give considerable weight to international issues.

3. *Specially designed courses, lecture series, or discussion groups.* These activities are sometimes labeled "noncredit work," "informal courses," or "adult educational programs," such

terms being used to distinguish them from customary courses or course sequences. These activities may be offered at any of the three locations used for regular courses or course sequences.

World affairs is one of the most common and recurrent themes used in planning special courses and series of this sort. The announcements of university extension divisions provide countless examples of courses with such titles as: The Soviet Union Today; World Politics; World Affairs Are Your Affairs; The United States in World Affairs; Ways to International Understanding; Pathways to Peace; and The United Nations. There are also many courses which relate to particular countries or areas of the world and to special problems or topics.

4. *Special activities (such as concerts, exhibitions, or lectures) provided on the campus for the members of the academic community and those who live near by.* At every university, this kind of service is provided on a more or less sporadic basis by all parts of the institution. In addition, there is often a special bureau or office to develop and coordinate such services.

Many activities of this sort are concerned with international issues simply because of the wealth of speakers and other resources in this field. Furthermore, campus groups concerned with foreign affairs often make a concerted effort to spread knowledge about their particular interests by scheduling special events. The University of Miami, for example, has a strong concern with Hispanic-American affairs; it schedules an annual lecture series on the subject, invites Latin-American artists to appear in concerts, arranges many special exhibits, and highlights the visits of distinguished Latin-American scholars. The Miami community participates in all these events. Some universities have invited outside groups to participate in the creation of the campus environment. Such is the case at the University of Pittsburgh, whose "nationality rooms," described in another volume of this series, are sponsored by interested groups in the city. These rooms provide the basis for a continuing program of meetings, conferences, dinners, and other activities. Many universities and colleges are in small towns and the campus programs become an integral part of the life of the community. In New Paltz, New York, for example, the State University Teachers College carries on an annual celebration of United Nations Week (including speeches, panels, conferences, mass media publicity, posters, films, and dramatic presentations) which is a joint campus-community venture.[1]

5. *Correspondence study programs,* offering both customary courses and specially developed programs designed primarily for adults. The National University Extension Association now includes fifty-three institutions which maintain such programs, some of them of great magnitude. The undergraduate and graduate courses now available include virtually every subject in the university curriculum.

World affairs is represented in this total offering in the same varied ways that it is on the campus. To suggest a few examples: six institutions offer courses on foreign policy; three, on international organization; six, on international politics; fifteen, on international relations; and six, on foreign trade.

6. *Short course and conference programs,* which bring groups of people together for intensive, full-time study for periods of time ranging from one day to several months. A number of universities are now using special centers on or near their campuses which combine meeting-rooms, dormitories, and arrangements for eating. Other institutions use hotels, estates, summer camps, or other available locations.

Many universities sponsor annual conferences on world affairs, usually choosing a central theme for each year. Examples of this activity are the Conference on American Foreign Policy at Colgate, the Institute on World Affairs and International Coopera-

[1] The enrichment of the extracurricular life of the campus is a central theme in another volume in this series. See Howard E. Wilson, *American College Life as Education in World Outlook* (Washington: American Council on Education, 1956).

tion at Pennsylvania State University, the Institute on the United Nations at Mount Holyoke, and the Annual Conference on World Affairs at the University of North Carolina. In addition, numerous short courses are organized around special topics of world affairs or are planned for groups interested in that subject. Some of these activities are advanced seminars; examples of this type are the American Assembly at Columbia and the Norman Wait Harris Institute at Chicago. Perhaps the widest coverage of all is provided in the lectures or other presentations which are included as one aspect of conferences devoted to other subjects. There are few topics for conferences which do not have some international implications, and a fairly large number of the short courses being sponsored by American universities take account of that fact. As a balancing or leavening measure, many such courses include talks or presentations on general topics, frequently on world affairs.

7. *Radio programs,* over a university-owned station or stations or offered on time contributed by a commercial station.

University stations faced with providing many hours of programs each week often use world affairs as a continuing or occasional theme for courses, panel shows, analyses of the issues behind the news, and reports on the international situation as it affects the interests of special groups of listeners, such as farmers. Most of the stations also use programs prepared by the National Association of Educational Broadcasters and distributed by its so-called "tape network"; these programs frequently deal with international relations. National coverage is also secured by a few programs which are broadcast on commercial networks. The Northwestern University Reviewing Stand, for example, often uses international topics as themes around which to build its weekly discussions.

8. *Television programs,* offered in one of three ways: over a university-owned station; over a commercial station which contributes time; or over a cooperatively developed educa-

tional station which the university does not own but which depends on the university for some programs.

The situation with respect to television is similar to that with respect to radio, except that, because educational television stations are usually not controlled by the universities themselves, the programing is not so directly a university responsibility. In this situation, many universities are making their distinctive contribution by putting on the air modified versions of regular courses, some of which are concerned with world affairs. At the University of Michigan, for example, telecourses on international relations have been offered on the University of Michigan Television Hour.

9. *The provision of instructional materials to groups or individuals.* These materials include: films, records, pictures, other audio-visual aids, books, pamphlets, and packaged libraries.

All of these materials contain a great deal of information about world affairs and provide a wide range of sources for persons interested in study in this field. A number of universities have been designated as information centers for the United Nations, the American Association for the United Nations, and other agencies or associations and, therefore, receive quantities of materials to disseminate. At many universities particular efforts have been made to build specialized materials services around international relations. The University of Indiana, for example, has published a guide, *Selected Films for World Understanding,* for the use of groups wishing to sponsor programs in that field.

10. *Programs designed to aid local communities to analyze and solve their problems.* Usually an individualized consultative and developmental program is offered by the university, working with and through the leadership in communities which request the service.

Ordinarily these programs are immediately concerned with local problems and result in direct action designed to solve them. In the course of the discussions, however, some groups develop an interest in topics which lead naturally to a better understanding of world affairs. The University of Nebraska and the University of Virginia, for example, both regard their community-development activities as fruitful channels for building world understanding. Also, as a result of community-development programs, local groups or institutions often decide to organize their own adult educational activities. The University of Washington finds that foreign affairs is the chief topic with which such local groups are concerned.

11. *Programs developed to aid special occupational groups,* such as engineers, teachers, lawyers, architects, librarians, school administrators, or civil service employees of various kinds. In the case of the professions, the appropriate college or school which provides preservice training usually directs the off-campus program, often collaborating with the extension division. In the case of the other occupations, the extension division itself usually maintains the program.

Since virtually all these groups, and particularly the professions, are vitally affected by international relations, it constitutes one of the common topics for their educational programs. International trade, for example, is a frequent theme for conferences of businessmen. Many workshops are held for teachers and educational administrators who wish to introduce more content about world affairs into the school curriculum. Furthermore, in general conferences designed for these occupational groups, some consideration is given to international matters.

12. *The Cooperative Extension Service* is actually but one illustration of the previous category, but it has developed such a strong tradition and broad scope that it deserves special mention. It was initiated under the terms of the Smith-Lever Act

of 1914, and its present budget is now in excess of $100 million a year, derived from national, state, and local sources. It is an integrated service chiefly for farmers and homemakers. Traditionally it has been vocational in character but with a broad concern for all aspects of rural life. It provides trained educational workers for virtually every rural county in the United States and is now rapidly expanding into urban and suburban areas. Within each state, it is administered by the land-grant college, with some coordination being exercised by the U. S. Department of Agriculture.

Since the Cooperative Extension Service is markedly decentralized, its program is determined locally, with stimulation and help from the administrators and the subject-matter specialists at the land-grant colleges. Therefore, the concern with world affairs varies considerably in terms of the nature of locally felt problems and the concern felt by state and local personnel. In general, however, a substantial amount of work is being done in world affairs education. Farmers often feel themselves to be in direct competition with foreign producers both at home and abroad, and on this thread of interest a number of efforts to create better understanding of world affairs have been built. The discussion of public problems is an important part of the work of local groups and also assumes marked prominence in state-wide meetings, such as the Farm and Home Week, held annually at the land-grant college. There has been a substantial exchange of agricultural workers among countries, and the Cooperative Extension Service has used these contacts to the full to help educate citizen groups. Rural associations are also assisted to build programs dealing with world affairs. One of these groups, the Associated Countrywomen of the World, is entirely devoted to the idea of international understanding and has gained considerable strength in a number of states. World affairs education is not the central focus of the Cooperative Extension Service, but, because it is the most highly developed adult educational program in the country, it exerts a more widespread influence on world affairs understanding than does any other single university program.

13. *Services provided for other public or private institutions,* such as prisons, sanitariums, and welfare institutions. Here the university assumes responsibility for all or part of an educational program in such institutions.

In such services, world affairs education is usually merely an incidental part of the activities provided in generalized programs.

14. *Educational programs designed particularly for the university's alumni.* Usually these activities are provided on a generalized basis for all graduates of the university and are sponsored by its alumni office or secretary. Sometimes, however, there are specialized groups of alumni of particular departments or programs within the university. Increasingly, in fact, the adult educational programs (particularly the course sequences) are developing their own alumni groups. Alumni educational activities include the introduction of lectures and demonstrations into homecoming and anniversary celebrations, the sponsorship of reading courses and discussion groups, the scheduling of faculty speakers and panel discussions before alumni clubs, the use of alumni publications as media of education, and the development of special programs to meet the interests of particular sections of the alumni group.

Many alumni programs include some activities related to international relations, particularly where the faculty in that field are able and articulate or where the alumni secretary is concerned with the increase of knowledge about world affairs. At Miami University (Oxford, Ohio), for example, the executive secretary of the Alumni Association believes that it should take an active part in promoting an interest in world affairs because every college graduate has a duty to keep informed about current world problems. A four-day Alumni College has been developed, and other activities are proposed.

15. *Specialized program services for clubs and associations.* Many local and state-wide citizen groups turn to the university for assistance in building their educational programs. The program service bureau may go to great lengths to help develop coordinated courses, discussion outlines, packaged materials, and leadership training aids.

Such associations are often interested in international relations or can be led to have an interest in that subject. The University of Wisconsin, for example, has long been noted for its program services to groups, and these include many vigorous efforts at world affairs education. Alabama College (Montevallo, Alabama) maintains a club program service for outside groups, particularly women's organizations; some of its study programs have dealt with: "Trouble Spots in Today's World," "As Others See Us," "The United Nations," and "Communism: What It Is." Many universities provide organizational and developmental services for outside groups, and frequently these are centrally or partially concerned with international relations. The State Organization Service of the University of Minnesota, for example, has a very highly developed program of this sort. In 1954, it had 19 affiliated organizations with a total membership of 116,796; most of these organizations had active international relations programs.

16. *Speakers bureaus,* scheduling faculty members and other persons for engagements away from the university. These engagements may be for speeches, forums, panel discussions, or other kinds of group presentations.

One of the most popular subject-matter areas of these bureaus is foreign affairs. The 1954 announcement of the bureau at Rutgers University, for example, listed 59 speeches in that field which its faculty members are prepared to give, in addition to talks on travel, literary, artistic, and cultural subjects. Many of the other speeches listed undoubtedly include some consideration of international matters. Occasionally speakers bureaus concentrate some or all of their efforts on foreign affairs. A good example is the

Institute of International Affairs of the Oregon State System of Higher Education. Ever since World War II it has provided speakers and forums to the people of Oregon. In one four-year period it reached 60 communities and had a total audience of more than 40,000 people, not including those listening by radio.

17. *The production or publication of educational materials,* such as films, audio-visual aids, books, and pamphlets. The university presses are the best known means of issuing materials, although they do not usually think of themselves as being adult educational agencies. However, many other production services operate either as continuing programs or sporadic efforts.

Here, as in the other generalized adult educational services, world affairs is one of the recurrent themes. Materials in this field are produced occasionally or frequently in terms of the sense of need for them.

18. *Organized services for foreign students and visitors to the campus* in which these students are used to heighten local understanding of their countries and the problems of world affairs.

Large numbers of foreigners now visit university and college campuses for brief or extended periods of time. In many parts of the country, such students or visitors are the only people from abroad whom local residents have any chance to meet or know. As a result, most institutions now have a more or less highly developed program of scheduling such visitors to speak to groups, to visit in homes, and to maintain other formal and informal contacts. Michigan State University, for example, has long sponsored a program of "Community Adventures in World Understanding," in which foreign students go into Michigan communities in a carefully organized schedule of visits, discussions, observations, and interpretations, designed to serve both the foreign students and the participants at the community level. The university also sponsors a "Christmas Adventure in World Understanding," which involves 100 carefully selected foreign students from American colleges and universities and approximately 600 families, as well as governmental, social, civil, and industrial agencies. Some nation-wide programs for foreign visitors, such as the International Farm Youth Exchange, are administered in each state on the land-grant college campuses. The program of collaboration set up between American and foreign universities by the International Cooperation Administration has also brought to American campuses a number of foreign faculty members, who are often used to help build local understanding of the problems of their countries.[2]

19. *Sponsorship of leagues or competitions* concerned with music, art, drama, forensic, or other interests. Most of this work is done with young people, but some of it involves adults.

These competitive activities are only occasionally concerned with international relations.

20. *Consultative or reference bureaus,* either general or in such special areas as education, business, engineering, or municipal government.

All of these bureaus handle matters dealing with international affairs, particularly questions of world trade or governmental structure or operations.

21. *Organized tours,* in which an educative content or focus is given to a program of travel.

Foreign travel for adult groups under university sponsorship is growing rapidly. Organized tours and general cultural seminars held in foreign locations are perhaps the most frequently found forms, but specialized programs for teachers, businessmen, labor union officials, public employees, farmers, and other groups are sometimes offered. New York University, for example, annually

2 For further analysis of foreign students, see Cora Du Bois, *Foreign Students and Higher Education in the United States* (Washington: American Council on Education, 1956).

conducts a number of such specialized activities. In addition, many universities (chiefly in the East and the Midwest) are now sponsoring tours to the United Nations either for the general adult public or for specialized groups. Many of these tours, either abroad or to the United Nations, include lectures, discussions, readings, and other interpretive and educational activities.[3]

Adult Education as a University Function

The general view of university adult education which emerges from the foregoing enumeration of the major services rendered is one of great variety. But even in those institutions in which adult educational service has been well established for a long period of years, it does not yet enjoy a status of complete equality with other university activities. Some programs may have very high prestige, but others are merely tolerated and are permitted to remain only so long as they pay their own way or produce substantial public relations dividends. On every campus there are some faculty members who perennially raise the question whether adult education is an appropriate function for the university, often implying that it is not. Most extension deans know that, in any period of necessary financial retrenchment, they would have more difficulty in defending their programs than would their fellow deans.

The reason for this situation is, of course, that service to adult students is a relatively recent function of a university and is, therefore, not yet fully accepted by those who wish to hold to tradition. Actually the true tradition of the university is one of growth and change. The university began as a means of training young men to carry on a life of scholarship. Later it took over from chivalric institutions the education of the leaders of society and from various other institutions the training for the professions. In the twentieth century it has assumed a far broader series of functions, extending both its subject matter and the range of

[3] For a further discussion of tours, see Wilson, *op. cit.,* pp. 141–65.

young people whom it serves. Substantial direct service to adults started about 1885, but did not become extensive until the second quarter of the twentieth century. Thus it is difficult to find in the university's history a period which can be cited as the golden era of stability of function, unless indeed one goes all the way back to the early beginnings in the Middle Ages.

When university adult education first begins on any campus, no question of its appropriateness as a function usually arises, primarily because the initial program of service usually meets some immediate and readily apparent need. It is only later, when there are a number of activities and they have broadened out into a generalized pattern of services, that murmurs (and even shouts!) are heard. By then, of course, the work is firmly established. Particular programs may be abandoned from time to time, but each one is usually replaced by several others.

A large part of the generalized opposition to adult education arises from antagonism to particular activities. A faculty member or an administrator observes an extension division or an evening college providing some service which he believes to be beneath the dignity of a university. Taking the part for the whole, he criticizes a broad function on the basis of some particular expression of it. Here, it may be said, sound grounds for complaint sometimes exist, for, in their effort to establish their work, extension deans have occasionally sponsored activities which they themselves could not defend with any enthusiasm. It is true that the adult educational services are not the only parts of the modern university in which excesses have occurred, but the existence of a few inferior courses in a graduate school or a college of commerce is usually not made the basis for an argument that that part of the university should be abandoned. There would seem to be no reason why a similar suggestion should be made about the general extension division.

The basic resolution of the question of whether or not adult education is an appropriate university function must come from the efforts of those who are responsible for planning and administering it. To the extent that they can formulate and apply standards and principles of service worthy of an institution of higher learning, their work will speak for itself. No matter how good it is, however, it will never manage to escape substantial criticism, chiefly because a university, like any other complex organism, is a system of tensions and balances. The time-hallowed battlegrounds of academic life are still fought over daily: the humanities versus the sciences; liberal education versus professional training; the old versus the new professions and subject-matter departments; the pure versus the applied sciences; education for all young people versus education for the ablest few; and all the other issues which are constantly—and often fruitfully—discussed and argued. To their number, the modern university adds one more: the issue of the "regular" versus the adult student. In all these areas of constant controversy, balances are somehow achieved, although they shift from time to time. The question of what forms of adult education are appropriate for a university can never be answered for all time. It will be discussed and decided again and again on campus after campus.

The Organization of Adult Educational Services within a University

As a university develops its services for adults, there usually comes a time when they grow too large to be regarded any longer as a miscellaneous assemblage of particular activities scattered throughout the institution. At this point, two basic policies come into conflict. The first grows out of the need to consider adult education as an extension of the whole university, with the careful preservation of the right of the respective departments and schools to establish and maintain the standards which their subject-matter or their professional responsibilities dictate. The second policy springs from the need to coordinate the work in the field so that there can be a proper focus and balance of services in terms of the needs and interests of the mature clientele, and so that the resources of the institution will be used carefully and economically. Every university must somehow work out a balance between these two general policies.

No two universities have worked out the same balance, and none of them is satisfied with the pattern that it now uses. The literature on university adult education is filled with analyses of the problem of how the university may best organize itself to discharge its adult educational function, but so far the questions raised vastly exceed the answers that have been found. Perhaps the best way to indicate the dimensions of the problem is to suggest something of the diversity which now exists.

In Oregon, there is a unified system of higher education, incorporating all public institutions of higher learning. This system includes a separate Division of University Extension, whose director is responsible to the chancellor.

At the University of California, which is also a unified system, there is a vice-president for university extension. But there is also a vice-president for agriculture, and it is to him that the Cooperative Extension Service is responsible.

At Michigan State University, there is a vice-president in charge of Continuing Education Service, who is generally charged with coordination of all adult education throughout the institution.

At many state universities there is a general extension division, with a dean or director reporting to the central administration of the institution and coordinating most of the adult educational functions. At no state university, however, are all educational services for adults administered by the dean or director, the most usual exclusion being the extension services of some of the professional schools, including agriculture.

Many urban universities include an evening college, headed by a dean or director. This college usually includes many, but not all, of the educational services for adults.

At New York University the various divisions and schools operate their own credit programs of adult education, but there is, in addition, a Division of General Education which provides a very large array of non-credit activities.

At Harvard, each part of the institution operates its own adult educational program, although there is a general series of courses, the sponsorship of which is shared by other universities in the Boston metropolitan area.

In Florida, which has a unified system of higher education, a single extension division serves all public institutions in the state, but its dean is responsible directly to the president of the University of Florida.

This oversimplified account of existing institutional patterns does little more than suggest the range of the existing diversity. Perhaps it will suffice, however, to demonstrate how impossible it now is to specify any blanket prescription about what should be done. Once again the answer must be left to the future and to the evolutionary development that must occur on each separate campus.

One conclusion may be advanced with some certainty. The problem of achieving a balance between the two conflicting policies cannot be solved by organizational means alone. Each of the two principles identified above demands the exercise of power. The first would decentralize that power, and the second would concentrate it. No structural pattern can be devised which will automatically compensate for all the differences of emphasis and influence which characterize the modern university. There are always jurisdictional and personal concerns, on the one hand, and strong desires for a comprehensive approach, on the other. Some forms of organization provide for better, more integrated, and more responsive operation than others, but no pattern is adequate to solve all the problems.

At least part of the answer must be found in improved administration, in the building-up of established and accepted policies of procedure rather than of systems of authority. In each institution there must grow a strong tradition of adult educational service, at once integrated and flexible, based upon a general adherence to established policies but a willingness to revise and change them in the light of new developments. It is only when effective administration of this sort is coupled with sound organization that a university can begin to discharge its adult educational function with full effectiveness.

The patterns of future service will be extensions and developments of existing forms, not radical departures from them. Four kinds of effort which are already well established will continue simultaneously. First, present programs of adult education will be extended and enlarged. Second, universities that now provide only limited services will broaden them to include more of the activities that are now under way at other institutions. Third, better coordination and integration of services will be brought about. Finally, the inventiveness of university educators of adults will continue to lead them to create new forms and new methods by which the public can be given a better understanding of all aspects of life, including those which have to do with world affairs.

CHAPTER SIX

Arousing the Interest
of the Inattentive Citizen

THE FIRST TASK of the university educator of adults as he plans a particular program is to define the nature of the audience he hopes to reach. As was pointed out in chapter 3, the general public may be broadly categorized into four groups on the basis of its knowledge about, and concern with, world affairs: the inattentive citizen, the attentive citizen, the actively concerned citizen, and the specialist. In this chapter and the three which follow, each of these groups is examined to discover its distinctive needs for learning, the general method of approach which may be used in educating it, and the special role of the university in that education.

Who Is the Inattentive Citizen?

The central fact which all proponents of world affairs education must face is the apathy of the inattentive citizen. More than a hundred million American adults are dispersed across the country in countless kinds of groupings; sometimes it almost appears that all they have in common is their disinclination to apply their minds to the sustained contemplation of international relations. Seasoned observers were not surprised when Martin Kriesberg estimated that only 25 percent of the people showed any knowledge of foreign problems.[1] The only question was whether that figure was not too high.

[1] Kriesberg, "Dark Areas of Ignorance," in Lester Markel and others, *Public Opinion and Foreign Policy* (New York: Published for the Council on Foreign Relations by Harper & Bros., 1949), p. 51.

The inattentive citizen is so faceless—or, rather, has so many faces—that it is hard to see him at all, much less make an estimate of how to change him. Nonetheless, it is possible to discover certain very broad and general ways in which he differs from his neighbor who is concerned with foreign affairs.

The closest approach to a profile so far constructed is that drawn by Almond.[2] By concentrating on those aspects of his study which relate to knowledge of world affairs as revealed by the data derived from sampling polls, it is possible to reach certain broad conclusions.

With respect to *age*, there are no profound differences, but there is a tendency for the inattentive citizen to be older than the attentive citizen. As Almond puts it: "The younger groups are likely to set a greater priority on international affairs than on domestic," and "they are likely to be more informed on the organizational aspects of international relations."[3]

There are substantial differences with respect to *sex*. Women are apparently less attentive than men to matters of foreign policy. To quote:

. . . more women than men seem to be ignorant of or apathetic to foreign policy issues. There are consistently more "don't know's," "no opinion's," and "undecided's" among women. The differences in this regard are quite high, ranging from 10 to 20 percent.[4]

The women who are attentive, however, tend to be more idealistic than the men.

Income is also related to attentiveness. In the upper-income group, 28 percent belong to groups or organizations which discuss national and international problems as compared with 16 percent in the middle-income group and only 8 percent in the lower-income group. When asked whether they thought that there is

2 Gabriel A. Almond, *The American People and Foreign Policy* (New York: Harcourt, Brace & Co., 1950).
3 *Ibid.*, p. 118.
4 *Ibid.*, p. 121.

something the United States could do to prevent a war, 10 percent of the upper-income group gave "no opinion" or "don't
know" as their answers as contrasted with 13 percent of the
middle-income group and 22 percent of the lower-income group.

Occupational grouping is so closely connected with income that
it is natural that the two would have a common pattern. As
Almond says:

> . . . professional persons and executives . . . are the most informed
> sector of the American population, the most interested in foreign affairs,
> the least pessimistic about the prospects for peace, and the most opti-
> mistic with regard to the capacity of the United States to develop policies
> which might prevent war. At the other end of the scale, unskilled and
> semiskilled labor, domestic servants, and farmers are the least informed
> group in foreign policy matters, the least interested in international
> issues, the most pessimistic about efforts to maintain peace, and the
> most inclined toward nationalist and isolationist attitudes.[5]

Before World War II *regional variations* may have been substantial, but now they do not appear to be pronounced, particularly so far as attitude is concerned. Almond found, however, that
in the late 1940's "on questions involving information about
foreign affairs, the Middle West and particularly the South seem
to have lagged behind the other regions."[6]

Rural-urban differences are more clear-cut. To quote once more:

> The rural population is less attentive to problems of foreign affairs.
> They have less information on world politics: fewer of them belong to
> organizations in which foreign affairs are discussed. More of them were
> "undecided," or refused to express an opinion when confronted with
> foreign policy questions.[7]

The sharpest differences are related to *education*. When the re-
spondents to public opinion polls are analyzed into three groups
on the basis of formal schooling, the differences in their answers

[5] *Ibid.*, pp. 124, 126.
[6] *Ibid.*, p. 132.
[7] *Ibid.*, p. 132.

are often striking. Four examples of this sort[8] will portray vividly
the relationship between attentiveness and education:

	College	High School	Grade School
Percent who show a reasonably correct understanding of what a tariff is...........	64	50	22
Percent who belong to groups or organizations which discuss national and international problems......................	32	15	7
Percent who gave "No opinion" or "Don't know" answers when asked whether they were satisfied with the progress of the United Nations.......................	8	21	32
Percent who gave "No opinion" or "Don't know" answers when asked their opinion concerning reciprocal trade agreements...	10	24	49

The picture which emerges from Almond's careful study is a
familiar one to social scientists since it clearly conforms to the
general pattern of differences which has so frequently been found
between those who are informed on many different subjects and
those who are not. Inattentiveness to world affairs corresponds
in its general configuration to inattentiveness to diet, safety, vocational efficiency, and other areas of human concern. There are
no surprises, no strange reversals of relationships. To be sure, in
all such collections of data the social scientist deals only with very
general bases of differentiation, and Almond stresses particularly
the great overlapping among the basic groupings. It is entirely
possible that an elderly, impoverished, uneducated farmer's wife
in the South may be deeply concerned with world affairs and a
young, well-to-do, male lawyer in New York City may be completely inattentive toward them. The chances are, however, that
the situation will be reversed.

The Educator and the Inattentive Citizen

There are, in general, two ways by which educators react to the
fact that a relatively few concerned and interested people are

[8] *Ibid.*, p. 129.

surrounded by so many others who appear to be sunk in lethargy.

Some would argue that, if this situation has gone on for so long, it must be a natural order of affairs. Why, then, give it thought? Those who are already interested certainly require more education to learn what they want to know. Let them continue, and broaden the pattern of activities which meets their needs, cordially welcoming all who wish to join them. In that way, those who plan educational programs can devote their attention to the essentials of content and method. Growth will occur, but only as a natural process when newcomers are attracted by the quality of such programs or when the conditioning influences of life give more people an interest in their own improvement.

This view is anathema to all those who are moved by logic or temperament to urge the spread of enlightenment to all mankind. To them, a fundamental task of modern education is to extend knowledge to a constantly larger number of people. Until the middle of the nineteenth century, for example, the majority of the inhabitants of even the most civilized countries were illiterate. Observers in those days often suggested that an inability to read and write was a natural condition, borne out by all history and made manifest by the disinclination of the masses to do anything about their ignorance. The widespread literacy of today has not been brought about by holding to an educational pattern designed for an interested elite but by vigorously developing and spreading new programs to involve increasing numbers of people. If the values of widespread participation in world affairs are ever to be achieved, they must be sought in the same fashion.

However convincing either traditionalism or reform may be made to appear rhetorically, few people ever act wholly consistently in terms of either. The cool rationalizer of the present situation wants, at least occasionally, to have a larger audience for his own words or for some project in which he is involved, and the ardent exponent of the expansion of enlightenment never really expects to reach the very last person among the hundred million American adults. Furthermore, both positions are similar in accepting the fact that in a democratic society more education is desirable. Nonetheless, the difference in viewpoint remains, influencing both theoretical discussion and practical action.

Much of the discussion has been based on several assumptions, more or less explicitly stated, each of which contains some element of the truth but which, in their total effect, tend to circumscribe thinking and cause it to revolve endlessly in certain predetermined patterns. Since these beliefs often act to inhibit invention, they should be examined and their truth assayed.

One assumption has been that people become interested in world affairs education only because they feel some responsibility as citizens. As a result, most appeals or exhortations directed toward the inattentive have concentrated on this motive among the many which move men. The feeling of social responsibility is indeed a powerful incentive, but it is far from the only one. As the analysis of existing programs in the previous chapter has shown, the approaches to the creation of interest are many and varied. Moreover, the sole reliance on civic duty as an incentive often indicates a failure to think directly about the specific groups at whom programs should be aimed. It is assumed that, because all adults are citizens, they will all be reached by this appeal. Actually, this assumption is too general; it lumps everybody together, thereby ignoring the countless individual variations which are of such great importance in building a sense of personal or group involvement.

It is also sometimes assumed that interest is created or intensified only by overt action or the possibility of such action. The lack of interest in world affairs has often been excused on the ground that there is little that the individual citizen can do about them. Activity does indeed build interest, but it is far from essential. Experts in recreation deplore the great increase in the popularity of spectator sports, which are given that name precisely because they permit no activity at all on the part of those who are so deeply interested in them—no activity, that is, other than discussion, the use of the mass media to keep up to date, and occasional observation of the spectacle itself. (For that matter, millions of Americans follow major league baseball who never see a game.) All these forms of participation are possible with world affairs, where the spectacle is far greater, more filled with human interest, and more directly relevant to the future of every citizen than is any sport.

The attempt to link up world affairs education entirely with activity and to suggest that learning is worthless unless the participant does something about it may actually hinder growth of interest. Knowledge and understanding are good for their own sake. The child knows what the adult sometimes forgets: that wonder and curiosity are natural traits of man and that their satisfaction needs no excuse. Every adult who analyzes his day's activities will find that he performs many acts which seem to bear out his desire to know, without any thought that the knowledge will be useful in some later connection. Why else does he read the newspaper, listen to his favorite commentators, follow up points in a conversation which he understands imperfectly, or consciously try to keep up with the latest plays, books, or movies?

It is sometimes maintained that interest in a subject is inversely proportionate to its complexity. Since world affairs are extremely complicated, the argument runs, only a small number of people will ever be able to develop a concern for them. It is doubtful whether this assumption has great validity. One of the essential elements of an enduring interest is its capacity continually to challenge those who possess it. Anybody who persistently follows a sport, or the doings of Hollywood and Broadway, or a hobby amasses a truly amazing range of facts and insights about it. When an intriguing murder trial, a sensational congressional investigation, or a devastating hurricane are in the news, the public has an insatiable appetite for information.

What is actually intimidating about the complexity of world affairs is the fact that usually so little satisfaction is provided for those who are beginning to be interested in the subject. They are confronted at once with the whole complex range of the subject and are not aided and encouraged by any sense of mastery over even the most elementary matters. A fundamental principle of teaching holds that the student must be given a constant sense of accomplishment, particularly in the early stages of his study. At the very least, he should have the feeling that he is grappling with fundamentals, that he is getting to the heart of the subject. It is time enough later on for him fully to understand what he has already sensed: that the very complications of the subject make it all the more interesting and significant. But he will never arrive at that later stage unless his learning experiences occur in the proper developmental and psychological order. It is the task of the educator of adults to build programs which will provide this kind of progression.

Strategies of Spread

Anyone who answers affirmatively the question of whether or not the educator should try directly to reach the inattentive public must develop some theory about the way in which interest in world affairs can be created. Since the number of inattentive citizens is so large and since they typically belong to the groups in society which have always been most resistant to education and change, a special strategy must be devised to reach them. Those who have thought seriously about the problem in the past have tended to borrow from the social sciences some central concept or integrating principle which might serve as a general guide. At least six major courses of action have been advocated.

THE INCREASE OF INFORMATION

The first and oldest strategy is merely to increase all the information-giving and educational services. When people who believe in this policy are asked what they desire of world affairs education, they answer simply, "More of it!" The specialists in international relations must advance their claims in competition with all those who want the attention of the citizen to be devoted to other problems. Let them, in effect, increase their clamor. This strategy has of late fallen into disrepute. Almond's skepticism about the value of campaigns of public enlightenment expresses the general view:

A discriminating analysis of the evidence suggests that a large sector of the lower-income, poorly educated majority of the population is incapable of assimilating the materials of informational campaigns. Its basic apathy is a consequence of emotional and social conditions. Its intellectual horizon tends to be quite limited, and its analytical skill is rudimentary. It will take a great deal more than public relations to remedy such a situation and produce the degree of involvement and activism which is characteristic of the upper educational and income groups. . . . Persons who tend to be objects of remote decision and manipulation in their private lives are unlikely to approach problems of public policy with a sense of mastery and independence.[9]

The National Opinion Research Center study in Cincinnati (described in chapter 2) provides an objective verification of this view.

As social scientists have come to understand somewhat better the level of education of the general public, however, they have wondered if information-giving has had a fair test. Are the facts being provided in such a way that the inattentive citizen can comprehend them? According to the 1950 census, the average American adult has had between nine and ten years of schooling, but most newspapers and magazines are written at a level of complexity which presupposes a considerably more advanced level of education. Often their stories on world affairs have a higher than usual readability index. To expect most men who have had only a ninth-grade schooling to read Walter Lippmann is like suggesting that the average third-year piano student should undertake a Beethoven concerto. Neither has the technical skills to accomplish the task. If the information about world affairs could be presented through the media which the inattentive citizen uses and in such a way that it is interesting and understandable to him, without distortion or making the news merely superficial, the

9 *Ibid.*, p. 130.

possibility of reaching the minds of a larger number of people would be greatly enhanced.

AUTHORITY

A second major strategy is to use the authority of outstanding individuals. The proponents of this course of action argue that if a recognized leader urges the public to study foreign relations, the public will respond by doing so. This method works very well when the leader has great authority, when he obviously has a strong sense of involvement himself, and when those to whom he speaks are near enough at hand so that he can appraise their response. When the president of a labor union becomes deeply concerned with helping non-Communist unions in Europe, for example, his immediate staff and the others who are close to him are likely to follow his example. Similarly, an influential and popular member of a club or other fraternal organization can often stimulate many of its members to focus their attention more directly on international relations.

As the possibility of immediate contact decreases, authority grows less effective in creating interest. The man who speaks from a public platform, no matter how influential he may be, has a task of communication which grows more difficult as it grows more general. He must have an extraordinarily powerful personality and a markedly fresh viewpoint if he is to reach and stir the minds of his audience. In doing so, he must avoid the excesses of exhortation, or even incantation, to which some speakers on world affairs are subject; as Almond says, they "have the virtues and failings of evangelism."[10] The central difficulty in the use of authority by mass means, however, lies in the fact that the inattentive public is usually so occupied with its own immediate concerns that it does not pay attention to any appeals which come from afar. When the President of the United States speaks on international relations over television and radio to the whole country, his words are heard and heeded by his listeners chiefly

[10] *Ibid.,* p. 6.

in terms of their already existing awareness of the importance of what he is saying.

The educator of adults who wishes to use the strategy of authority must realize that the authorities to whom many inattentive citizens listen (when they listen at all) are themselves not yet concerned about foreign affairs. The maker of opinion among the uninformed may usually be found in their immediate environment and occupies his place as leader more by reason of personality than position. The task of identifying and influencing him is therefore a first essential in the use of the strategy of authority.

INTEREST GROUPS

The third major strategy is to work through interest groups. Its advocates point out that one of the most significant characteristics of our society is its development of massive social aggregations built around common concerns. The pressures exerted by such organizations have a profound influence on the determination of both foreign and domestic policy. It is through unions, through industrial and commercial associations, through veterans, farmers, parents, and service groups, and through other organizations like them that American public opinion is formed. Many of the inattentive public belong to such groups and can, apparently, be approached only through them. Leaders of world affairs education will be wise, therefore, to try to use voluntary associations as a means of education. Join them. Work within them to spread a broader and more balanced view. Attach to the interest of the present association an interest in world affairs. If the group appears blind in some respect (which, perhaps, represents most narrowly its own interest), try to find in what respects its vision may be broadened.

The great potentialities of this strategy are somewhat harder to realize than at first appears. Many inattentive citizens have only token membership in the interest groups to which they belong. Within any large organization, the weight of influence is felt and exercised by only a small percentage of the membership, the rest being stimulated to action only by a crisis (such as the threat of a strike in a union) or a significant ritual (such as attendance at church on Easter Sunday). Furthermore, it is usually hard to stimulate an organized interest group to enlarge its policy because most people belong to it for the specific and practical reasons which are already expressed in its program. Moreover, the proponent of world affairs education must often compete for attention with the representatives of many other special viewpoints, each of whom has joined the interest group to try to influence its policy and program. None of these obstacles present insuperable barriers; they merely indicate the complexities and difficulties which must be faced by those who hope to reach the inattentive public by working through interest groups.

ELITES

A fourth strategy suggests that within every social grouping there is a cluster of people who, because of dedication, deep concern, inherited position, wealth, education, personal power and attractiveness, titular leadership, or control of media of communication, have a disproportionate prestige with their fellow men. The effective course, therefore, is to identify the people who constitute an elite and seek to educate them, knowing that they, in turn, will educate others. Ideas flow down channels of influence; the trick is to find the place where the channels begin and start the education there.

This strategy resembles the previous two in that it accepts both the factor of authority and its operation through interest groups. The elite, however, is a generalized and collective leadership with pervasive rather than specific influence. The strategy of using elites rests, in fact, upon a special (and, its proponents insist, realistic) view of the stratification of society. However, many of the problems found in pursuing the second and third strategies are also encountered here, and there is one major difficulty in addition: elites like to remain elite. More than one local world affairs council, for example, began by enlisting the social leaders of the community— and still has extended its membership no further. Those who try to influence an elite, unless they are firmly situated within it themselves, may find that it influences them! But when an elite can be brought to want to use its ascendancy, it often achieves great power in arousing the attention and interest of others.

The three last-mentioned strategies have the common element of working in and through established social patterns. The remaining two are alike in suggesting ways by which those patterns should be changed.

COMMUNITY DEVELOPMENT

The fifth strategy rests upon the belief that the local community should become the focus of common social effort in world affairs education as in other respects. In recent years, there has been a reaction against the segmentation of society by special-interest groups and an insistence that ways must be found to cut across them and find an orientation which is at once more general and more immediate. The community-development movement seeks to build a situation in which the pooled efforts of people in groups small enough to be subject to individual influence and large enough to be truly representative may lead to a better social order. Thomas R. Adam, for example, has suggested that education in international relations should start with local concerns. "When the world casts its shadow over a community," he says, "the householder's first thought is for the safety of his home and not for the future of the globe."[11]

According to the proponents of this strategy, the actual involvement of the inattentive citizen will be achieved in several ways. Through concern with local governmental problems, he will eventually gain an understanding of the nature of all government and, therefore, an appreciation of international relations.

[11] Adam, *Education for International Understanding* (New York: Institute of Adult Education, Teachers College, Columbia University, 1948), p. 21.

Local organizations concerned with world affairs can combine their efforts and thereby undertake programs which have a more significant effect. As community participation makes people more generally alert to their need for education and understanding, a greater number will take part in every kind of learning activity, including that which is concerned with international relations.

The community-development movement will almost certainly have a powerful impact in the years ahead, particularly as it devises techniques by which to enlarge the scope of the immediate concerns of those who take part. The citizens who begin with problems of local government, however, have a long road to travel before they get to international relations. To integrate local organizational efforts, which have been proceeding along separate pathways for years, and to build a social climate which stimulates people to want to broaden their horizons are not easy assignments. Once again, however, these difficulties merely suggest problems which must be solved.

GROUP PROCESSES

Those who propose the sixth strategy place their emphasis on the powerful effect of group processes. Modern man, they argue, is too anonymous and too prone to accept ready-made opinions. The development of bigness in every form—cities, industries, unions, political parties, voluntary associations, interest groups, media of communication, and all the other phenomena of modern life—has brought new benefits to many people and has created a previously unparalleled standard of living. But, say those who advocate the sixth strategy, as more people come into political life, they do so increasingly as automatons, with views shaped by their conditioning, with little sense of personal responsibility, and with restricted alternatives of choice. The inattentive public is large, and the general mood of the country is highly variable simply because there is no rooted stability. The educator must, therefore, try to counteract bigness in all its forms and must focus his attention on the building of small groups which can meet and discuss international issues together. The attentive public will grow, although probably only very gradually, because some people who are originally concerned merely with social participation will gain an interest in ideas. International affairs will be far better understood by participation in discussion. Most important of all, the group experience will help some people to develop an active concern for foreign affairs, and they, through their infinitely various personal relationships, may interest many others who might never otherwise participate.

Here, too, there are limitations and problems to be solved. Most people join groups because they are interested in purposes, not in association itself. As Almond's analysis has shown, furthermore, large numbers of the inattentive belong to segments of the population which do not find group activity either attractive or easy. Their interest must be very powerful and usually very specific to overcome their reluctance to join organized groups. Moreover, those who find it easy to belong to groups usually have a great many activities from which they may select. And, finally, groups, like elites, often tend to be clannish.

Despite these limiting factors, however, the use of groups has certainly been an important factor in increasing the size of the attentive public so far, and there is no reason why it will not continue to be significant in the future.

The Creation of Interest

These six strategies do not exhaust all the proposals which have been made, but they are the ones which are most widely advocated today. Each of them has its own ardent proponents who are convinced that it is the best pathway to the enlightenment of the general public. And yet, in actual practice, all six tend to merge together because fundamentally they all exemplify a single principle: *to create a new interest, attach it to one which already exists.* Each strategy is, in essence, not a plan of action but the selection of one basis of interest on which to build: factual information, the weight of authority, existing organizational involvements, the prestige of elites, community spirit, or the attraction of social participation in small groups.

The identification of the basic principle of interest creation makes clear the fact that the values inherent in the six strategies merely begin the list of interests which can be made to lead naturally and directly to a concern for world affairs. The range of other possibilities stretches out endlessly. But how does the movement from one interest to another take place? Perhaps the best way to answer this question is to examine how the connection occurs naturally. How did those citizens who are now attentive or actively concerned about world affairs first become interested in the subject? The authors have, in fact, raised this question with a great many such citizens and have invited competent observers to speculate on the subject. The answers, although by no means unanimous, tend to conform to certain patterns. In addition to the operation of the six strategies, there are certain other commonly found ways in which adults have developed a concern for international affairs. The following list is only illustrative, and it is not presented in any order of importance.

The attentive citizen may have had a good grounding in international relations as part of his formal education. His broad aim then was to secure a general education; as a necessary or optional requirement, he studied world affairs and still retains a residue of interest in the subject. Usually this study occurred during youth, but it may also have been undertaken in adulthood in connection with a degree or certificate program in an evening college, an extension center, or a correspondence division.

The attentive citizen may have developed an interest in world affairs as a result of a sense of commitment growing out of his ancestry. The very large number of Americans who still feel some sentimental tie with a foreign country are sometimes led by that fact to become especially sensitive to its policies and its position in the world. Often their interest is highly localized, and it may be narrow and bigoted, but that result does not necessarily follow.

A concern with one other country can be a bridge toward a more general interest in international affairs.

The attentive citizen may have come to fear war, nuclear weapons, foreign-trade competition, or other dangers. As a result of this fear, he has been driven to a study of what he and his country can do to avoid the dreaded ills. Some experts in health education have concluded that a relatively small number of people are interested in health but that everybody is interested in disease. Perhaps something of the same conclusion might be drawn about the field of world affairs education.

The attentive citizen may have realized that he can adequately fulfill the conditions of his employment only by developing a better knowledge of international relations. Both private industry and government need more and more persons who can deal with foreign affairs. The satisfactory performance of their present jobs and their hope for advancement rest in part on their capacity to understand and deal with international issues.

The attentive citizen may have a deep and absorbing personal interest in one of the arts or sciences. Such an interest, although seemingly irrelevant to foreign affairs, often leads to an awareness of the international aspects of such fields of interest as the dance, music, literature, or physics. A striking illustration of this point is the growing concern of scientists with the free flow of information in their fields.

The attentive citizen may have been forced by social pressure to develop an interest in world affairs. If his associates in his professional or private life are concerned with international matters and make him feel ignorant or uninformed because he cannot participate fully, he may be driven, sometimes despite himself, to begin to take an interest.

The attentive citizen may have been led to an interest in world affairs through a continuing and conscious attempt to broaden the base of his knowledge and understanding. The counselor in any adult educational agency can attest to the fact that this motive is more common than is generally realized. Men and women (usually in their late thirties or early forties) come to his desk to say, more or less frankly, that they feel that the routine of their daily lives has limited their horizons. They have, perhaps, had only a technical education, and they have followed it with a life which has had to be wholly absorbed by the need to get ahead on the job, to raise a family, and to find a basic social orientation. When these tasks have been performed, a broader and richer life should loom, but somehow the adults concerned find themselves inadequate to plan it or to lead it. Their general dissatisfaction does not always light on the field of international relations as a specific area of deficiency, but often it does. They do not understand what is going on around the world, they say. Perhaps if they knew, they could do something. But mostly what they want is to know.

The attentive citizen may have been stimulated by a need to learn how to discharge the practical but nonvocational responsibilities which fall to the lot of every adult. In performing many of the roles mentioned in chapter 1, some familiarity with foreign affairs is required. As a parent (perhaps of a son in military service abroad), as a wife (perhaps with a husband in the foreign service of government or industry), as an elected member of a political body, as a leader in a church, a union, a trade association, a service club, or some other voluntary organization, and, as a voter, the attentive citizen may realize the need for an understanding of world affairs. Also a contact with an agreeable foreign person is itself often a source of interest.

This analysis of motive could continue at great length, but it would be pointless to try to inventory all the incidents, impulses, chance occurrences, or special traits of character which might lead to the study of foreign affairs. The illustrations afforded should, however, be adequate to demonstrate the general principle of interest creation and, in connection with the previous discussion, permit several general conclusions to be drawn.

First, in order to interest the inattentive citizen, it is necessary to identify him, not in general, but in particular—as an individual or a member of a specific and distinctive group. Only if his present concerns are known is it possible to enlarge his viewpoint and increase his understanding. Second, the adult educator must use all the ingenuity and resources at his disposal to attach the new interest to the old. Third, the attentive public can probably best be enlarged by the gradual extension of present frontiers and the more intensive and imaginative use of motivations that have been successful in the past. Some method may some day be devised by which it will be possible to reach out and engulf whole new segments of the population, but until now a gradual and developmental program has proved more rapid. The educator of adults does not need to take the hardest and most resistant cases first. He can move slowly toward them, enlarging the attentive public wherever he can, with the hope that his efforts will contribute to a change in the total climate of opinion which will in turn help him interest those who, at the start, lie beyond his reach. Finally, the range of possibilities in the creation of interest appears far wider than has previously been thought. The creation of interest is never easy, but the approaches to the task are numerous.

The University and the Inattentive Citizen

Since the citizens who are inattentive to world affairs are so markedly differentiated by their relative lack of formal education, it may be argued that the effort to make them attentive is not a responsibility of an institution of higher learning. It is but one of countless adult educational institutions, many of which have more direct and intimate contact with the inattentive than the university can readily achieve. Furthermore, the attempt to reach this group is costly and time-consuming. It could quickly use up all the limited resources of a university, leaving none for the other three groups, which may well have a greater claim to its services since they have fewer alternate means of meeting their own distinctive needs.

A deeper view of the matter, however, indicates that the conclusion suggested by the foregoing arguments is too sweeping. The university must indeed be careful not to dissipate its efforts by a general and widespread attempt to reach the inattentive. But the five principles listed in chapter 4 as guides for the university as it develops its program suggest that it has a proper, indeed a vital, role to play in awakening the interest of those who are not yet aware of the significance of world affairs. If it plans its work carefully, the university can, in fact, be far more successful with a relatively small effort than it ever could if it went all-out in a general campaign to arouse their attention.

Not all inattentive citizens are members of that group in society which is most characteristically inattentive. As we have seen, attentiveness is more closely identified with formal schooling than with any other major factor which Almond analyzed, but even the college-educated group contains a number of people who are not informed about world affairs; 36 percent of them, for example, do not have a reasonably correct understanding of a tariff. If the university wishes to work with the inattentive, therefore, it does not need to discover ways of interesting those who have had little schooling. It can start with its own alumni and with all those other citizens who have a sufficient educational background to permit them to undertake university-level work easily and readily.

The most frequently used method for reaching this group is to introduce material on international relations into a program which is basically oriented to some other purpose. The group served by that program is already attentive to its purpose, and often the existing interest may be enlarged to include world affairs. Naturally, the success of this process of transfer is directly related to the actual relevance of the two interests and the skill with which that relevance is made apparent. The heavy-handed introduction of a speech on the United Nations into a conference on industrial time-and-motion study may well create more resentment, confusion, or boredom than enlightenment. The Co-operative Extension Service has been particularly skillful in some states in bringing to local agricultural commodity groups first an awareness of world markets and then a concern with the whole subject of world affairs. It has been equally successful in some localities in relating the rural homemakers' interest in family living to the patterns of domestic life abroad and then, on that base, broadening the range of concern to include a more general understanding of international relations.

At the State University of Iowa, this method has reached the status of an established principle in the operation of the Iowa Continuation Center. The policies of the center are made by a faculty committee, which early laid down the rule that persuasive efforts should be made to introduce elements of general and cultural education into conferences that might otherwise be of a purely technical or vocational character. This policy has met with some success. Such groups as the Iowa Nurses Association and the unions now make a regular practice of including some phase of international affairs in their programs.

A variant of this device is to introduce some feature designed to catch the interest of the inattentive in programs aimed particularly for the attentive, the actively concerned, or the specialist. An institute on international affairs, for example, may consist chiefly of seminars and discussion groups requiring a relatively sophisticated approach. It is a fairly standard practice, however, for such an institute to include one or more general public meetings addressed by its most distinguished leaders, relying on the attractiveness of their names and positions to draw some people who might otherwise not come.

Another method by which universities reach the inattentive is by designing programs which make a surface appeal to some other motive or interest but which are basically focused on world affairs. An example of such an activity is the conducted study-tour which a number of extension divisions organize, most typically to the United Nations. Some of the people who participate may be attracted by the prospect of an inexpensive trip to New York, shared by congenial company and mixed with a liberal amount of entertainment and recreation. During the tour, however, and in the meetings which may precede or follow it, they come to have a strong sense of the significance of international organization.

These two methods are directed chiefly toward the natural and typical clientele of the university adult educational program. In addition, a number of institutions have tried on an experimental basis to formulate programs which would reach into new segments of the population, particularly those which are made up of the more typically inattentive citizens. Often these programs are carried out in collaboration with other agencies of adult education or with voluntary associations. In such experimental programs, the university serves as an innovator, using its special knowledge of both subject matter and educational methodology to devise, construct, evaluate, and perfect a new program which can then be carried to a large number of people by the agencies or associations with which the university collaborates.

An excellent example of this approach was the "Great Decisions" program carried out in Oregon during the spring months in 1955. Nine basic issues were identified, fact sheets were written on eight of these issues (the ninth being deliberately left open), and an integrated program was devised to present the issues to the general public. The essential elements in this program included: a weekly television program in which the issue was presented, a weekly page on that issue in the Portland *Oregonian,* ninety-five voluntary discussion groups in homes or community institutions, and a weekly ballot which individuals could use to help them come to their own conclusions. This program was initiated by the World Affairs Council of Oregon, but it was carried out in collaboration with the General Extension Division of the Oregon State System of Higher Education and drew heavily on university faculty members for its intellectual leadership.[12]

One of the groups with which universities often have fruitful

[12] For further information about this program, see Frank Munk, "Oregon Makes Great Decisions," *Adult Leadership,* IV (1956), 18–21.

collaboration is organized labor. Here is a direct effort to reach a group in society in which inattentiveness to world affairs is frequently found. The University of Illinois, for example, has operated institutes for union members specifically in the field of world affairs. The University of Chicago has developed a special coordinated course entitled "Labor's Stake in World Affairs," incorporating textual materials, a discussion manual, and a specially designed leadership training program. This course was tested under field conditions and was then made available for use by the unions themselves within their own educational programs.[13]

In working with these outside groups and agencies, the university is essentially working not with the inattentive themselves but with those who are able to reach the inattentive. One such group is made up of people who work in the mass media: the editors and staff of the mass circulation newspapers and magazines, radio commentators and newscasters, writers, producers, and other personnel in the television and movie industries, leaders in the book-publishing field, and many others. The university can bring these people together and invite their consideration of some of the common responsibilities and problems they face. They do not need to be reminded that they are molders of public opinion, but they can be urged to reflect on the socially desirable objectives that can be realized through the media in which they work. In addition, the university has within its walls knowledge about the nature and shaping of public opinion, which it can convey. The public opinion and communication experts are in a position to report on the most recent research being done on public attitudes and behavior.

Thus, the university can here perform a function which no other institution is in a position to undertake. By a skillful blending of themes and persons, the university can contribute to the

[13] This course is described and other efforts to work with unions analyzed in Jack Barbash, *Universities and Unions in Workers' Education* (New York: Harper & Bros., 1955).

professional skill of mass-media specialists and can at the same time invite their reflection upon the meaning and value of the efforts in which they engage professionally. An example of this type of meeting is the conference held at the University of California at Los Angeles in June 1955 at which university professors and administrators, and representatives of all the mass media discussed many issues related to education and communication— and particularly the problem of interest creation—with great frankness and a subsequent general agreement that the conference had been profitable for all parties concerned.

Conclusion

The university educator of adults must always operate within his own known and specific community: the city, the region, or the state for which he feels some responsibility or which provides the best opportunity for his service. If he wishes to work in the field of world affairs, he must face the fact that his community usually contains a large number of inattentive citizens, who cannot be segregated or ignored. Inattentiveness often merges very gradually and imperceptibly into attentiveness, which itself has many levels of awareness and interest. In serving the whole community, therefore, the educator of adults must consider how he can best deal with all four groups—the inattentive, the attentive, the actively concerned, and the specialists—without ignoring any of them and without departing from the principles which should always guide university adult education.

The local orientation of each university educator of adults lends concreteness to his efforts. The inattentive public may have only a shadowy outline when it is viewed nationally, but, seen close at hand, its size and nature become far more sharply defined. As we have seen, it is necessary to understand present interests in order to create new ones. Only in the immediate and local community do such present interests become most sharp and clear. Operation within specific frameworks always imposes limitations of money, method, human resources, and potential audiences, which can be overlooked by those who speculate in the abstract and are not bound down by time and place. The demands of the immediate also give a concrete reality which is essential to any successful effort at enlarging the attentive public.

Most university educators of adults have concluded that there are no bold moves—or, at least, no moves that educators can make—that will at once enormously enlarge the number of persons interested in world affairs. They also believe that the creation of interest cannot safely be left to spontaneous generation. It is a legitimate part of the educative process and can best be undertaken by carefully identifying potential audiences (not the whole broad general public) and constructing programs of learning which will appeal to them. Progress may be slow, but it will be substantial. This process of planned expansion offers the best hope for making the inattentive attentive.

CHAPTER SEVEN

The Education of the Attentive Citizen

THE APPROACH to the responsive publics—the attentive, the actively concerned, and the specialist—is characterized by one overriding common factor. All three publics are, in varying degrees, *ready* for further education. The inattentive public is, by definition, unprepared to learn; thus, as the preceding chapter has indicated, all initial efforts to reach such adults must consist of attempts to arouse interest. But this precondition of learning already exists in the responsive publics. With them, the educator can concentrate on education rather than on attention-getting.[1]

In the latter part of this chapter and in the two which follow, some suggestions are offered for the education of each of the three responsive publics. Underlying all these proposals are certain fundamental propositions applying to adult political education, which are offered here as an introduction to the three chapters.

Underlying Propositions

The three propositions, each of which requires a brief explication, are these: (1) the objectives and the maturity of adults require and permit a markedly different plan of political education from that designed for pre-adult students; (2) a liberal education is indispensable to complete citizenship; and (3) world affairs education must be balanced with and related to other aspects of political education.

---

[1] This is no doubt an oversimplification. Educational offerings must arouse an existing interest among the responsive publics; conversely, attention-getting devices must also be educational if they are to make the inattentive attentive. But the basic difference in emphasis here alluded to is nevertheless fundamental.

1. *The objectives and the maturity of adults require and per-mit a markedly different plan of political education from that designed for pre-adult students.*

It will seem to many a natural and reasonable procedure to turn to the introductory course in international relations at the college level for a model which the evening college or extension division can imitate. In fact, in many institutions the identical course is taught in both places. There are several reasons why this practice falls short of the ideal means for educating the attentive public. These reasons proceed from the significant differences between the young college student and the adult with respect to maturity and with respect to educational objectives.[2]

For the college student, the introductory course in interna-tional relations is part of a whole educational program, more or less integrated, depending on the college. With rare exceptions, an adult course must stand by itself, since few adults have op-portunity or inclination for more than one course at a time. (A not inconsiderable number who are exceptions are those adults who are working for degrees in the evening college.) The college course is planned in a context of simultaneous reinforcement by other courses and, in addition, with the expectation of subsequent work along similar lines by many students. While it is true that the introductory course "is increasingly molded to serve the whole wide range of objectives of general liberal arts education at the undergraduate level,"[3] in many cases aspects of political problems of utmost importance are deliberately omitted from the introductory course in international relations because of a program which introduces these aspects at another point in the curriculum. Such omissions become gaping defects if carried over

---

[2] In addition, the introductory course provides a less stable guide than might be supposed, owing to the extensive revisions and experimentations which are now taking place. For an interesting discussion of these developments, see Vincent Baker, "The Introductory Course in International Relations: Trends and Problems," *Universities and World Affairs,* Document No. 62 (Mimeo-graphed; New York: Carnegie Endowment for International Peace, 1954).

[3] *Ibid.,* p. 9.

into an adult course lacking these complementary supports.

Similarly, there arises a conflict between a plan of study which is an introduction to a subject, presupposing further exploration subsequently, and a course which may be terminal for most students. This difficulty exists within the college introductory course itself. Vincent Baker, in his study of these trends, raises the question "whether the basic course, now considered as an *introduction* to the study of international relations, serves equally well as the best background in the subject for the student who will pursue no further studies in the field."[4] But the difficulty, if it exists at the college level, is much more acute in the case of the adult, for his interest is solely in the development of a citizen's understanding of world events, not in preparation for political science teaching or research or specialist training in international relations. The objectives of the students in the two cases, then, may very well differ; certainly the curricular setting and its objectives are quite dissimilar.

It has often been said by teachers of adults that the maturity of their students is the special quality which makes such teaching attractive and rewarding. In any subject field this maturity will have its rewards; in those in which an understanding of human nature and society are especially required, the rewards will be multiplied. Politics is such a field; the civics class in high school and the political science course in college often have an unreality about them that derives directly from the absence of experience and maturity in the students. The root questions in the social sciences are questions about human nature and conduct: "What is man?" "What does he seek?" "What form of society does he require?" What kind of government suits him best?" While these basic questions must be posed as soon as the student can cope with them, the practical implementation of human goals is a problem for the mature. The adult is able to take into account the conflict of interests, the accommodation of ultimate goals to existing circumstances, and such other elements as distinguish

4 *Ibid.*, p. 10.

politics from philosophy. Only the adult can test the wide variety of answers to these questions against his own experience and his own mature understanding of himself and his neighbors. Thus the adult program of education in world affairs can profitably afford to give more attention to these questions than can be given at the pre-adult level.

But it is not enough that the university *recognize* adult experience. It must also *interpret* it, *respect* it, and *use* it.

The adult comes to the university aware that significant events are taking place in the world. He hopes that the university will help him to interpret their significance and to relate them to his own understanding of his society based on his mature adult experience.

To say that the educator must respect this experience does not mean only that adults must be treated as adults. It means also that this experience must be respected as a body of knowledge or, more precisely, as the material for a body of knowledge. Political theory is built up from generalizations about that human species which populates adult classes of universities as well as the more numerous remainder of the population! Adult experience is something unique; it cannot be matched anywhere else in education. Is the university going to make it possible for the adult, for the teacher, and for the university itself to profit from this knowledge of life which it recognizes, interprets, and respects?

If so, it must use this resource. Not only must the university through the teacher bring its understanding to bear upon the student's experience, so that he can absorb this understanding and thus reinterpret and discover the meaning of his own experience; it must also adapt its methods so that the experience itself can be brought to bear upon the issues by the adult's participation. Thus, the use of discussion methods will be seen not only as a way of keeping the student on his toes, a way of testing his interest and his perception, a way of schooling him in the art of conversation, and a way of developing the other arts of communication, but also as a way of introducing the elementary materials of all theory and knowledge about human affairs—namely, human beings and human experience—into the educational setting.

2. *A liberal education is indispensable to complete citizenship.*

Liberal education is aimed at the perfection and completion of each individual man by concentrating on those aspects of the person which are uniquely human, and which make men worthy to be thought of as ends in themselves. Thus a liberal education is distinguished from vocational training and from any other sort of activity which concentrates on the development of aspects of the human being which make him merely useful, merely a means to some end outside himself.

By its very nature, then, a liberal education focuses attention on the *ends* of man and of society. Thus, a liberal education is indispensable to the citizen in the fullest sense, since it enables him to discover those ends which political activity, the means, serves. A free society is thought to be especially friendly to liberal education because it is understood by all that the state exists for the sake of the individual and not the individual for the state, and, therefore, that education is most appropriate which helps the individual to understand what purposes the state serves in making him better and happier.

This is all familiar; yet it seems to have unfamiliar consequences. For if the state exists for the sake of the individual, then *man as citizen exists for the sake of man as man.* There is a tendency in emphasizing the importance of developing good citizens to think of that development as the whole function of education. But citizenship is that aspect of man's life which relates to public affairs; and if the individual means something apart from the state and beyond the state and is more than a servant of the state, then man as a citizen is simply a part of his capacity to be fully a man. Since the democratic way of life is not an end in itself, the fundamental aim of a free society is destroyed if those qualities are not developed and cherished *for the sake of which* men are citizens. A liberal education is a means of discovering what those qualities are and how they may be acquired.

The argument has a direct application to foreign policy. If governments are established to enable men better to carry on their lives as individuals and as social beings, then the foreign policy of a government exists to create or preserve relations external to the nation which further enable them to pursue the kind of life they desire within their own borders. Thus, the purposes of men's individual lives and of their national life—what they seek, what they wish to be—must be clarified if their foreign policy is to serve these ends effectively.[5]

Liberal education, then, is more than relevant to citizenship. It is, in fact, a precondition of the best kind of citizenship, for the liberally educated citizen alone can judge the wisdom of policies, domestic and foreign, by their success in establishing conditions favorable to the pursuit of individual and national purposes.

Within the responsive publics there are many persons who have been to college and who therefore possess, in some degree, a liberal education. Nevertheless, the prevalence of specialized and vocationally directed education in the colleges, and indeed even in the high schools, in the last forty or fifty years has produced an adult population often unconscious of the liberal arts. What are the consequences of this for the university educator of adults?

First, some effort must be made to provide an integrated program of liberal education which takes into account the special character—both the peculiar opportunities and the limiting circumstances—of a mature and busy adult group. Quite different approaches, each worthy of attention, are to be seen in the program leading to a Certificate of General Education at New York University's Division of General Education[6] and the Basic Pro-

[5] For a perceptive development of this argument, see George F. Kennan, *Realities of American Foreign Policy* (Princeton, N. J.: Princeton University Press, 1954), chap. 4.

[6] *Courses for Adults*, New York University Bulletin, Vol. LIV, No. 2 (New York: Division of General Education, New York University, 1953), p. 43

gram of Liberal Education for Adults at University College of the University of Chicago.[7] Any further consideration of the problems and prospects of such a program is outside the scope of this volume, but the evening college dean or extension director may find fruitful a further study of these pioneering efforts.

Second, the university's program of world affairs education must be planned with a conscious relationship to an adult liberal education. There are at least two approaches which utilize this relationship. One is to develop such a program as a sort of "graduate" opportunity for those who have engaged in an intensive liberal education, either in college or in adulthood. While such a program will have the maximum value to those it reaches, it will of necessity reach only a very small audience. Another approach is to plan a course in world affairs in such a way as to introduce or reintroduce the idea of liberal education throughout; this plan will give breadth to the program itself and will have the effect of leading the participants into other educational activities which provide liberating experiences—literature, philosophy, and political theory, for example. Such a program will have broader appeal. One criterion of its success will be the extent to which participants actually move from it to other work in the liberal arts.

3. World affairs education must be balanced with and related to other aspects of political education.

Anyone attempting to state what the citizen needs to know about world affairs risks setting goals impossible to attain if he fails to take into account the limits set by the equal need to know about vital questions of public concern which are domestic in character. The educator must attempt to provide a balanced educational fare. The extension director and evening college dean will recognize at once that a well-rounded citizen education program should include problems of national, state, and local

[7] University College, University of Chicago, *A Basic Program of Liberal Education for Adults* (Chicago: The University, 1955–56).

concern as well as those of international scope. It is a cliché that foreign and domestic questions are inseparable, but it is true nevertheless. A recent report provides typical illustrations:

> One striking example . . . is furnished by a moment's reflection upon what a major economic depression in the United States would be likely to do to our foreign policy. Quite apart from its devastating effects on the personal fortunes of the American people, such a catastrophe might well mean the end of effective American assistance in the reconstruction of economic life throughout the world. . . .
> [Furthermore] those who have had experience in international conferences and conversations, particularly since the war, know that one of the most serious liabilities of the American position is the discrimination in the United States against some races and religious groups. When United States representatives at international conferences debate almost any question, what Secretary of State Acheson has called "the gap between the things we stand for in principle and the facts of a particular situation" is called to the attention of the conference.[8]

Overemphasis on foreign affairs not only neglects other important public questions but in fact distorts, by its partiality, the world problems under consideration.

Local communities are facing problems of crowded schools, teacher shortages, housing redevelopment, crime, and corruption. Many states wrestle with legislative reapportionment, water shortages, new sources of revenue, civil liberties legislation, fair-employment laws, and highway construction. Nationally we are confronted with problems of budget and taxes, racial integration, the national defense, efforts to curb the treaty-making power, immigration quotas, agricultural surpluses and price supports, wage-and-hour legislation, conservation of resources, trade policy, and a host of others. If public opinion is to exercise an intelligent and knowledgeable concern with these issues, even at the most general level, the attentive citizen must be equipped to reflect on such matters as well as on issues of foreign policy.

This wide range of public concerns illustrates the magnitude

[8] Educational Policies Commission, *American Education and International Tensions* (Washington: Educational Policies Commission of the National Education Association and the American Association of School Administrators, 1949), pp. 6–7.

of the educational task. An attempt must be made to discover the inescapably vital principles, facts, and ideas about foreign affairs which the citizen needs, for anything more may prove too taxing or too exclusive of other equally significant issues. This offers a formidable task but also a unique opportunity for the universities.

Beginning with the attentive public, an attempt must now be made to describe the characteristics of each class of responsive citizens, its needs in world affairs education, and the opportunities open to the university. The approach to the task will be based upon the three propositions outlined above.

Characteristics of the Attentive Citizen

The attentive citizen is, by definition, ready to learn. He has discovered problems and ideas beyond himself and his own career and family—public problems—and is willing to consider them. He may not possess a balanced judgment or a well-developed set of ideas and principles of international relations. Even his attentiveness may be accounted for by some concern other than the public interest; indeed, it may be a very special private interest—the tariff on wool or the fact of a relative abroad—which accounts for his concern. At the very minimum, what has happened is that he has seen the relevance of great events; he gives at least sporadic attention to the political occurrences of the day. Thus, becoming better informed, he moves into the "attentive public," separating himself, if almost imperceptibly, from the uninformed, inattentive mass.

Reference to the description of the inattentive public in the previous chapter[9] will disclose the characteristic differences between the inattentive and the attentive publics with respect to formal education, sex, geographic location, and other factors. In summary, it appears that the attentive public tends to be

---

[9] See pp. 79–82.

college-educated, middle- or upper-middle in income, urban more than rural. In addition, there is a tendency for men to be somewhat more attentive than women. Sex and residence factors are much less significant than economic factors, and the economic factors in turn somewhat less significant than differences in education.

Goals for the Attentive Citizen's Education

There are many ways of organizing a program of world affairs education for the attentive citizen. Many varieties of program, differing in method or in emphasis of ideas, will have their special values. But regardless of the way in which a specific activity is organized, it will, if it is well conceived, aim toward the development in the citizen of certain attributes of mind which provide the basic equipment he needs in order to think clearly and judge wisely concerning world affairs.

1. AN ABILITY TO FACE AND ASSESS FACTS

There was a time when it was commonly said, "Just give the people the facts and they will make the right decisions." One still hears this theme occasionally, even from political scientists, but it is not so common a prescription as it once was. There are good reasons for this change in attitude. The proposition itself, instead of illuminating, actually covers up the problem. For we have seen, in the first place, that there is no such thing as "just giving the people the facts"; most citizens will not receive them; they are the inattentive public already described. But even in the case of the attentive citizen, giving him "the facts" must presuppose some selection of facts. For there is no way that anyone, even the expert, can know all the facts relevant to any single major international problem; the amount of relevant factual material is in effect infinite.

Also the facts are constantly changing. A given collection of information acquired in college twenty years ago no longer describes the world of today. Even very important data—the relative strength of nations, their industrial potential, and their boundaries and forms of government, for example—have greatly changed. Thus, the importance of discovering some principles for selecting, simplifying, and orienting the facts hardly needs to be labored.

But it may be worth emphasizing that there is no way that the facts can be disregarded. There is at times a disagreeable toughness about facts which tempts one to distort or ignore them. But there is nothing helpful in such a reaction; facts are the realities which must be seen as clearly when they are thoroughly disagreeable as when they carry the most promising news. Facing the facts is perhaps a habit of character; it often takes courage. It certainly requires a kind of maturity. "Such maturity," as Walter Laves has pointed out, is "hard to attain [but] is no different essentially from the mature outlook we expect of adults in their conduct of private affairs and important public business. It consists in adjusting our behavior to the realities of situations."[10]

2. A CAPACITY FOR CRITICAL JUDGMENT

The development of the capacity of the individual to arrive at sound conclusions about a whole range of human concerns is, clearly, one of the main functions of education. The limits of this book do not permit an examination of the means by which this general capacity is developed but some consideration needs to be given to the specific meaning of this capacity in reference to world affairs. It would appear that a well-developed critical capacity with respect to world affairs would involve the following elements:

a) an ability to speculate about the consequences of a given foreign policy decision—what it might mean for this country, what reactions it may produce elsewhere, how it compares with other available alternatives;

b) an understanding of the limits of certainty within which

---

[10] Laves, "Some Essentials of International Understanding," *Adult Leadership*, July-August 1953, pp. 5–7.

decisions in foreign policy can be reached; an appreciation of the unknowable factors as well as of the more certain ones;

c) a willingness to consider only those alternatives which take into account the hard realities faced by the nation, and not fantasies based upon conditions as one might wish them to be;

d) an understanding of the way in which desirable goals may conflict in a particular situation; for example, in the case of the Korean War, the conflict between the desire to stop Communist aggression and the desire to stop fighting;

e) some forethought about the order of importance of the things one seeks, so that when such conflict arises, it can be resolved wisely;

f) an understanding of the limits of expert knowledge; a realization that, while an expert evaluation of the factual situation is necessary, policy recommendations will differ and they must be accepted or rejected on their merits;

g) an ability to pursue and to carry on a sustained argument, seeing the logical relation of premises to conclusions; and thus an ability to see the defects as well as the strong points in a chain of reasoning.

A program of world affairs education which aims to equip the citizen to meet his responsibilities can be tested in part by the success of its efforts to develop these specific abilities and understandings among those it serves.

3. AN INSIGHT INTO PERVASIVE THEMES IN FOREIGN AFFAIRS

Several important themes can be suggested which help to develop the capacity for judgment in the specific context of foreign policy and world affairs. No attempt will be made here to provide an exhaustive list. Those which follow are offered as examples of the types of themes which can have an important practical effect on the ability of citizens to think intelligently about world affairs. These are not topics for a course outline; rather they are pervasive themes which will appear and reappear in the consideration of world affairs generally and of American foreign policy in particular.

a) *The complexity of foreign affairs*

The comparatively sudden American involvement in vexing problems in all parts of the world seems to have produced two common, though opposite, reactions. On the one hand, a great body of the public has thrown up its hands and said, "It's too deep for me"; a smaller but more articulate group is prepared to offer its simple solutions, picking up some one single principle—whether it be America first, anticolonialism, peace at any price, the crusade against communism, or world government—and applying it as the sole test of our national behavior in every circumstance. Persons of the latter sort, being active in behalf of their beliefs, are more influential than those who despair of understanding. It is difficult to steer a course between the two, and yet that seems to be what responsible citizenship requires.

If each citizen were to make a list of the goals the United States should seek in the world, he would have no difficulty naming a good many on which most others could agree: peace, freedom to lead the kind of life one desires here at home, self-government as soon as possible for all peoples, the abolition of tyranny, lawful and friendly relations among nations, relief from the arms burden, a higher standard of living for the underprivileged peoples, and security from attack. Preparing such a list is a relatively simple task, but the complexity of world affairs becomes plain when these aims are placed against the practical issues before the nation. How do these goals help decide what to do about liberating the satellite countries, whether to support the South Koreans against aggression from the north, whether to recognize Communist China, what attitude to adopt toward Indian "neutralism"? Clearly, the goals sought are not irrelevant; ultimately they will determine policy. The complexity arises from the conflicting claims that these goals make upon foreign policy and from the limits of possible action that any single concrete situation places upon the government. Past commitments, as well as future hopes, must be weighed and measured.

The argument could be pursued further, but perhaps enough has been said to support the view that any genuinely educational effort must face up to the complexity of foreign affairs. For the sake of clarity, there is always a desire to simplify. But what value will there be in an approach which disguises, and thus distorts, the problems by making them appear to be simpler than they really are?

b) The limits of American power

The rise of American power in the world has been spectacular. Perhaps Americans have become overimpressed with it. Events since the end of the Second World War should, at any rate, give grounds for a reassessment of the nation's strength. The United States is the most powerful nation on earth. Is it then all-powerful? Since 1945 additional consolidations of power by Soviet Russia have occurred against American wishes. Partly in order to counter that threat, the United States has assisted in strengthening both West Germany and Japan until each is now a critical factor in the balance of power in its part of the world. Largely as a result of their own intense impulses, the peoples of Southeast Asia, especially India, Burma, Pakistan, and Indonesia, have assumed independent status and, with it, have become independent sources of power in world affairs. Chinese power is being consolidated under a new regime unfriendly to the United States.

In every problem this country faces around the globe—whether it be the unification of Germany, a settlement in Southeast Asia, or the restoration of trade between Japan and China—it is confronted by other interests willing to commit their power toward a solution which may be contrary to American interests. In some cases the nearness of local power and the remoteness of the power of the United States may be decisive. It follows from these conditions that this country is not always in a position to obtain what it seeks.

A tradition of great success marks the history of American diplomacy. This may lead Americans to expect from their government more than it can give. In the future, whatever a nation obtains in the world can only be got at great price. Responsible officials must always ask whether it is in the nation's interest to commit the manpower, the prestige, the money, the guns, and the bombs that it may take to gain what the people seek. In every case the responsible officials in the State Department must ask not only, "What are the facts in the case?" and "What would be the best solution for the United States?" and "Do we have the power to obtain that solution?" but also, "Is the cost worth the gain?" Responsible citizens, if they are to support and understand their government, must ask themselves the same questions.[11]

c) Morality and the national interest

Perhaps the most unique theme in the recent writings of American scholars and diplomats has been a debate over the morality of the use of power in the pursuit of the national interest. The debate has led to a fruitful re-examination of the purposes of foreign policy. Yet it appears that no comfortable compromise has yet been reached. On the one side is heard the argument that American preoccupation with ideals, such as those expressed in Woodrow Wilson's Fourteen Points, has obscured the central purpose of foreign policy, namely, the pursuit of the national interest.

It is argued in reply that the national interest must be broadly conceived, that idealism *is* our only real interest and its fruits our only real security. Are not American basic interests the same as those of free people everywhere? To this the answer is made that this country is better off, and will be better understood, if it tries only to figure out what *it* seeks, and to use its foreign policy to promote those aims. But isn't such a course selfish and narrow? Doesn't America's position of leadership in the world require that she raise a standard of good conduct worthy of her position? Of

---

[11] For a full development of this theme see Charles Burton Marshall, *The Limits of Foreign Policy* (New York: Henry Holt & Co., 1954).

course, it is argued in return, but morality in foreign policy requires that the conduct of that policy serve the citizens of the country concerned. So the argument runs.

In its many ramifications some fundamental questions are raised which deserve the attention of the thoughtful citizen: What is foreign policy for? Whom should it serve? What is meant by good conduct in foreign relations? Are there any real standards of measurement? What is "the national interest"?

d) The role of public opinion in the conduct of foreign affairs

An earlier chapter dealt with the role of public opinion as it affects the kind of education that is appropriate to the citizen.[12] While it seems necessary that the educator, as an aid to planning the curriculum, should have a clear conception of the role of public opinion in the conduct of foreign policy, it is equally urgent that the question itself should receive the attention of the adult citizen. For he will profit greatly from an attempt to determine the way in which his opinions and those of his fellow citizens should impinge upon the decisions reached by his government.

International relations, it has been argued, are too difficult and too remote for most people to understand. This position has been sharply put in an oft-quoted observation by Sir Alfred Zimmern:

The greatest danger which confronts our subject is to regard it as a subject for beginners. . . . It is this spirit, more perhaps than any other single cause, which has blocked the path of international understanding during the last fifteen years, both in the field of ideas and in the field of political action. The attempt has been made to simplify international relations, to clothe them in language intelligible to the man in the street, to enshrine them in attractive formulae, to reduce them to watchwords, even to enshroud them in a bewitching mysticism. . . . International relations are not simple; they are very complex. To simplify them is to destroy their essence, to eliminate the whole substance of the problems.[13]

[12] Chap. 3 (pp. 32–44).
[13] Zimmern (ed.), *University Teaching of International Relations*, A Record of the Eleventh Session of the International Studies Conference, Prague, 1938 (Paris: International Institute of Intellectual Co-operation, League of Nations, 1939), p. 11.

Granting that oversimplification is a disservice, is there a way in which the attentive citizen can come to grips meaningfully with these issues? If not, how is public policy to receive that corrective which comes from public scrutiny? In any case, so long as democratic government exists, foreign policy will sooner or later be judged by the people. The question is not so much whether foreign policy should be democratic; the question is: Being democratic, will it be wise?

The task, then, that the citizen must set for himself is constantly to examine the major questions of policy which confront the nation in order to discover *at what level* or *in what terms* he can make judgments about them. Sometimes he may conclude, as George Kennan did concerning the Indochina situation in 1954:

> There is little to be gained at this moment by any attempt to mastermind our government's actions, day by day, from the outside. This is an incredibly complex and baffling situation. We are now in it up to the hilt. The time has passed when any back seat driving can do any good. Our government is obviously making a concentrated and determined effort to come to grips with the problem. We can only wish them well and give them our confidence and support. There are times when, having elected a government, we will be best advised to let it govern and to let it speak for us as it will in the councils of the nations.[14]

Part of the citizen's wisdom will consist in knowing when and when not to take issue with the government's policy. It will be in the interest of the experts as well as in the interest of the citizen to have this knowledge, this capacity for discrimination, as widespread in the body politic as the resources of education can carry it.

4. A THEORETICAL UNDERSTANDING OF INTERNATIONAL RELATIONS

Among teachers of international relations, there is a widely voiced concern over the lack of systematic theory. It should be

[14] Kennan, *op. cit.*, p. 95.

emphasized that, if there is such a lack, this is not due to over-sight. Many theoretical approaches have been offered in a relatively short span of years, but apparently none has gained the unreserved acceptance of the teachers of international relations. This may also be said, in some degree, of all the so-called social sciences; that of itself does not dispose of the problem. The acuteness of the difficulty in international relations may very well arise from the fact that the subject is itself a compound of a whole host of special studies—geography, psychology, law, international organization, economics, history, sociology—some of which have an established theoretical stability, others of which have not yet been encompassed by an accepted structure of ideas. A theory of international relations must be a sound synthesis of many elements, although some of these elements have not yet themselves been satisfactorily defined.[15]

What is the purpose of a theory? In the simplest terms, a theory explains what happens. This is the function of theory in economics, in physics, in psychology, in biology. Theory gives meaning to events; it explains the stubborn facts. Theoretical development in the sciences generally results from the discovery of new facts which the current theory does not explain; a new effort at generalization is required in order to encompass those new facts.

A theory of international relations must explain the world situation; to the extent that it falls short of an explanation, it fails as a theory. Henry M. Wriston has expressed to the authors the opinion[16] that what we have seen in recent years is a series of attempts to organize ideas about international relations—international law, the historical approach, international politics, geopolitics, power politics, economic determinism, rationalism, empiricism, the psychological approach, etc.—each of which has somehow failed to explain the world situation. If the experience in other fields of human knowledge offers guidance, then men will not be content until they can explain the events that take

---

[15] See pp. 19–20.
[16] Interview with Henry M. Wriston, Jan. 20, 1955.

place in the relations between nations by reference to a coherent body of thought. The need for theory will be felt until it is met.

There is no need to explore the question of theory in detail here. The problem of the development of a discipline, which would provide a theory or theories, has already been indicated.[17] Clearly, if there were a generally accepted theory of international relations, an understanding of it would be the first order of business in the education of the citizen. In the absence of such a theory, the citizen needs to develop an understanding of the various attempts to fill this gap, to see their limitations, to test them against the events which require explanation. He will have to begin, in effect, to construct his own theory, tentatively and no doubt with misgivings. If he is wise, he will keep an open mind about many things, for he will appreciate that there is always more to absorb and relate to what he already knows.

A sound program of education will help him to construct a framework of his own, which will enable him to steer a course between the twin perils of a blind and stubborn dogmatism and the empty-headed uncritical temper, turning about with every new impulse, which often passes for an open mind. If the attentive citizen finds himself displeased with the incomplete and tentative set of ideas he is putting together for himself, he may find some comfort in the words of Somerset Maugham, who, upon looking back over his own mode of thought, offers the following description of himself:

> I am like a tramp who has rigged himself up as best he could with a pair of trousers from a charitable farmer's wife, a coat off a scarecrow, odd boots out of a dustbin, and a hat that he has found in the road. They are just shreds and patches, but he has fitted himself into them pretty comfortably and, uncomely as they may be, he finds that they suit him well enough. When he passes a gentleman in a smart blue suit, a new hat and well-polished shoes, he thinks he looks very grand, but he is not so sure that in that neat and respectable attire he would be nearly so much at ease as in his own rags and tatters.[18]

[17] See pp. 15–19.

[18] W. Somerset Maugham, *The Summing Up* (New York: New American Library, 1938), p. 160.

What the Universities Provide

What do the universities now offer to help develop these attributes of mind among attentive citizens? Most of the activities described in chapter 5 on "The Scope of Present Services" reach the attentive citizen, but for the most part they have not been planned with a particular concern for his special needs. Thus, one does not find a full range of activities, each designed to develop one or another of the particular attributes described above. The programs now mentioned are a selection of activities which seem to exemplify some, but not all, of the purposes appropriate to the education of the attentive citizen.

Accurate and rounded factual information about current developments in foreign affairs is provided by many colleges and universities through a variety of means. Lecture series, such as those offered by the Social Science Foundation at the University of Denver, are perhaps still the most common means of meeting this need. The lecture has its limitations, but when well done it provides a concise and authoritative review, as well as skillful interpretation. In addition, when the lecture is given by a government official—the Secretary of State, an ambassador, or a lesser officer—one has the opportunity of making a personal assessment of the quality of the public servant, though it must be admitted that such presentations usually suffer from the restrictions, multiple authorship, and lack of candor which almost necessarily accompany official utterances. Some institutions have attempted to meet the need for information through less formal devices. An example is the community program of Orange Coast College in California, which has developed a pattern of weekly meetings including a survey of the background of a particular movement or area of tension.[19]

The attempt to develop capacity for critical judgment through reading and discussion of basic problems in world affairs has

[19] For a brief account of this program, see Giles T. Brown, "Two Minutes Are Not Enough!" *Junior College Journal,* XXV (1954), 75–82.

been made more recently. The World Politics Program—with its introductory series based on serious and fairly extensive readings, followed by two other and similar series on American and Russian foreign policy—began in 1947 through the sponsorship of University College of the University of Chicago and the Chicago Council on Foreign Relations in cooperation with the American Foundation for Political Education. It is now offered throughout the United States under the sponsorship of colleges, universities, public libraries, school systems, and religious and civic organizations.[20] Though the program has grown and prospered, it has tended to reach mostly the upper level of the attentive public and the actively concerned.

Its very success illustrates the need for developing, in addition, less demanding programs for the less attentive. Attempts of this sort include the Great Decisions program[21] and the film-discussion program of the Fund for Adult Education entitled "World Affairs Are Your Affairs."[22] In many cases these programs have reached the same public; in other instances the local sponsors have succeeded in developing an audience which includes the less attentive.

Another development of interest is the concentrated study of areas of the world, providing a thorough examination of the political, cultural, and economic character and problems of a particular area. The variety of such efforts range from the annual Institute on the Far East and World Affairs at Oregon State College, which has very successfully involved community organizations of all sorts in the college town, Corvallis, to the ambitious Slavic Areas Program used in several extension centers of the University of Alabama.

The importance of liberal education to an understanding of

[20] American Foundation for Political Education, *A Statement Including the Annual Report of the Executive Director for the Year Ending June 30, 1955* (Chicago: The Foundation, 1956), Appendix II.

[21] See previous reference, p. 100.

[22] The Fund for Adult Education, *Annual Report: July 1, 1954 to June 30, 1955* (Pasadena, Calif.: The Fund [n.d.]), pp. 17–19.

world affairs has already been stressed. Perhaps the best example of an attempt to bring international relations within an adult program of liberal education is found at City College of New York. Its new associate in arts program offers a two-year plan which includes a group of courses designed "to further understanding of the cohesive and disruptive forces at work among the important areas of the world."[23] This group is prescribed "on the presumption that this aim is basic in general education."[24]

Many other examples could be mentioned. The attempt to uncover the strengths and deficiencies of present programs will be made in the final chapter as part of a general assessment.

Great opportunities for pioneering await the educator of adults who will study and understand the characteristics of the attentive public and who will then build a program based upon that public's educational needs and interests. He will find it necessary to take into account those fundamental propositions outlined at the outset of this chapter. In addition, he will need to focus upon those goals which are especially appropriate to the education of this group: an ability to face and assess facts; a capacity for critical judgment; an insight into pervasive themes in foreign affairs; and a theoretical understanding of international relations. In addition, he will profit from a study of the most interesting programs now available. The need is acute; the possibilities of distinctive success are open to the discerning educator of adults.

[23] City College of New York, "The Associate in Arts Degree," Administrative Committee Meeting, May 7, 1952, Calendar No. 15 (Mimeographed; New York: The College, 1952), p. 1.
[24] *Loc. cit.*

CHAPTER EIGHT

Serving the Actively Concerned

THE THIRD PUBLIC, the actively concerned—distinguished from the inattentive and the attentive, discussed in the two previous chapters, and from the specialists who are considered in the following chapter—is a relatively small group, but eminently worth the careful nurturing which the university can give.

Who Is the Actively Concerned Citizen?

The actively concerned citizen has certain distinguishing marks which set him off from the attentive citizen, though the two are very much akin. He is even more attentive; world affairs are not just one of a number of public issues which occasionally engage his attention; for him foreign affairs are of sufficient importance to call forth a constant and intense concern. In addition, he is typically a leader in efforts to persuade others that they too should feel the urgency of this interest; and he is often actively engaged in efforts to gain adherents for his views or fellow-members in a cause.

The actively concerned public includes members of the boards of directors of local world affairs councils and of the Foreign Policy Association; chairmen of foreign policy committees of independent voters' organizations; international relations chairmen of women's organizations; members of foreign trade committees of chambers of commerce; discussion group leaders in the World Politics Program; members of local study groups of the Council on Foreign Relations; certain political party officials; certain Army and Navy officers, such as those who attend the war colleges; and officers in the foreign departments of large banks. Into this group also fall a large number of persons whose affiliations are of a different sort, though they may often overlap the above classifications. These are the leaders of organizations of all sorts which offer special solutions to the problems of war and peace or in one way or another attempt to influence legislation in matters of foreign policy: the American Friends Service Committee, Facts Forum, American Association for the United Nations, United World Federalists, American Veterans Committee, Women's International League for Peace and Freedom, Federal Union, the American Legion, Americans for Democratic Action, and scores of others.

Many actively concerned citizens also display their interest in more informal ways. They are not "joiners," but they study the questions of foreign policy with care and discuss them with their friends. The influence of such persons may be very profound since it is based on intimate associations; in some cases it may even reach as many individuals as does the influence of an organizational leader, for interpersonal associations are powerful transmitters of opinion. One man influencing eight or ten friends, who in turn convey at least some shades of his opinions to a number of their friends, can thus be a significant social force.

The actively concerned public, then, includes a great diversity of persons exercising leadership in a variety of ways. The university educator of adults needs to bear constantly in mind, when thinking about his efforts on behalf of the actively concerned, how wide a range of persons make up this group.

How Can the Actively Concerned Public Be Enlarged?

Despite its diversity, the actively concerned public is a small group. It needs to be enlarged. This does not mean that it is a necessary goal of a democratic society that *all* citizens should have an active concern for world affairs. There are many other areas of public policy requiring an equally concerned body of interested citizens. Furthermore, a democracy can function admirably if the numbers of attentive citizens increase substantially, while a smaller proportion than at present remain inattentive and some increase occurs among the actively concerned. But this latter group, because it provides the means of transforming the other two larger publics, is the fulcrum on which success turns.

Where do the actively concerned come from? They are developed most often, no doubt, from among leaders within the attentive and inattentive publics. All actively concerned citizens are leaders, if the term is construed broadly to include both those who exercise influence through positions in organizations and associations and those whose influence is conveyed informally and intimately. But not all leaders are actively concerned with respect to foreign affairs.[1] The commander of a local American Legion post may happen to be uninformed and indifferent concerning questions of foreign policy; thus, he belongs to the inattentive public with respect to foreign affairs. But because he holds a position of leadership, an awakened interest in world affairs would quickly transform him from an inattentive to an actively concerned citizen. The transition is even easier and more natural in the case of a leader who is already attentive. A junior chamber of commerce president who is interested in problems of foreign policy becomes actively concerned almost without sensing the transition, because the role is so consistent with his habits of thought and leadership.

Some actively concerned citizens are no doubt drawn from non-leaders among the attentive public. Here, however, the interest in the problems or the sense of their urgency must be so

---

[1] In this book the division of the publics into four main groups (chapter 3) cuts across leadership. Almond and others have distinguished the publics in terms of the *policy-making process;* thus Almond has, in effect, a set of two groups of followers, the "general" public and the "attentive" public, and two groups of leaders, the "opinion elites" and the "official policy leadership." Gabriel A. Almond, *The American People and Foreign Policy* (New York: Harcourt, Brace & Co., 1950), p. 138. The division in this book is made in terms of *interest and understanding,* as has seemed appropriate for an analysis of the problem from the standpoint of education. Although all actively concerned citizens are leaders (by definition), leaders may be inattentive, attentive, actively concerned, or specialists.

great as to overcome passive habits and induce a new willingness to assume leadership, of either the formal or the informal sort.

The educator of adults will find, then, that in his efforts to enlarge the actively concerned public, his best hopes lie among the attentive leaders, the inattentive leaders, and the attentive non-leaders, in that order. He must adapt his approach to the interests and needs of each of these three groups.

How Can the University Serve the Actively Concerned Citizen?

The university can well afford to take pains with the actively concerned citizen, since, as a leader, he affects the understanding and interest of many others through his position of influence. In what ways can the university be of help? It can increase his knowledge of world affairs. It can help him harmonize his thoughts and his actions. It can increase his ability to educate himself independently of the university. It can clarify his particular role so that he understands it better and fills it more consciously and adequately. It can provide a rallying point for him and his fellows, giving guidance and stability. Each of these tasks can be described more fully and with illustrations.

INCREASING KNOWLEDGE

Actively concerned citizens do not necessarily possess a well-balanced fund of knowledge about foreign affairs. One finds in this group a wide range of information and understanding. At one end of the scale there will be an enthusiast who believes that he has discovered the key to all the world's problems; he never knew very much about foreign affairs and he doesn't see the need to learn any more. At the other extreme there will be the highly sophisticated, knowledgeable, and well-balanced citizen who can even step into the ranks of the specialists if the occasion arises— and sometimes it does.

Because of these differences, the educator cannot assume that the actively concerned citizen's education begins where the attentive citizen's leaves off. On the contrary, he may find that in a majority of cases the actively concerned citizen has the same basic educational needs as does the attentive citizen. These needs must first be met before the citizen can carry on with any special activities uniquely suited to his active concern. The first principle would appear to be: provide for those actively concerned citizens who lack them the basic educational programs which have been prepared for the attentive public; develop the ability to face and assess facts, a capacity for critical judgment, an insight into pervasive themes in foreign affairs, and a theoretical understanding of international relations. These attributes of mind are surely as necessary to the actively concerned as to the attentive citizen.

Beyond this there are opportunities for development of a more profound knowledge through concentrated educational offerings. The actively concerned are, by definition, more ready and willing to engage in intensive work than any other segment of the lay public. One plan which shows promise is the residential seminar. In a setting which permits uninterrupted and relatively intense concentration, and with the aid of specialists, general knowledge shared by a great many is brought to bear upon a particular complex problem of foreign policy. The Midwest Seminars on American Foreign Policy, sponsored by the Universities of Michigan, Wisconsin, Illinois, and Minnesota, are illustrations of such programs. In the second annual seminar in September 1955 about sixty citizens and about twenty specialists met for five days in the isolation of a lodge in the northern Minnesota woods to discuss the problems of United States policy toward Germany. Most of the persons invited to this conference fell into the class of the actively concerned public; some were invited almost solely because of their positions of leadership and influence in their states. The Colgate University Conference on American Foreign Policy, which has met annually each summer since 1949, relies heavily for its program upon official government representatives—ambassadors, counselors, United Nations representatives, and party leaders. The setting again is residential, and the specific audience is the community leadership, mostly of the Middle Atlantic states.

Opportunities of this kind serve several purposes. Within a short period of time they develop among the participants a substantial increment of knowledge about a particular problem. In consequence they also have the effect, for most citizens, of providing a new appreciation of the complexity of public problems when dealt with in all their concreteness and immediacy. In addition, they create reciprocal understanding between the lay citizens and the specialists. The specialists confront a segment of "public opinion"; the citizens see the specialists at work.

A more general sort of educational program would seek to open up and reveal the basic problems and principles underlying specific political issues. It would also be distinguished from the type of program suggested for the attentive citizen by its intensity. For example, in a general background program for the attentive citizen, a sketchy discussion of the causes of war might occupy one evening's work. But for the actively concerned citizen a series of ten or twelve meetings on this subject might be arranged. In the course of this series the most penetrating books on the subject might be read in their entirety. At the end of the series the citizen would have an excellent grasp of the problem, approaching in its scope, if not in its thoroughness, the understanding of a scholar.

Similarly, comprehensive studies might be planned around such subjects as diplomacy, international organization, the roots of American foreign policy, international economic policy, and nationalism. This is undramatic, serious education. Little has been done along these lines in the adult field. The programs that have been developed have received little attention; undoubtedly they attract only a few participants. But as the actively concerned public is enlarged through increased success in motivating attentive citizens, this sort of activity should prosper. Twenty adults engaged in such intensive studies may well be as valuable as five hundred who are superficially and sporadically engaged in another activity.

Then there are always some few keenly interested adults who would like to abandon all other pursuits for a time and come to the university to absorb all the learning they can. For them an occasional evening class or institute or discussion group is not enough. They would like to come onto the campus itself and to live the full intellectual life that it offers. But the university interposes many obstacles. Winston Churchill recounts the story of an effort he made in his younger days:

> . . . I had the idea that I must go to Oxford when I came back from India after the tournament. I was I expect at this time capable of deriving both profit and enjoyment from Oxford life and thought, and I began to make inquiries about how to get there. It seemed that there were, even for persons of riper years like myself, examinations, and that such formalities were indispensable. I could not see why I should not have gone and paid my fees and listened to the lectures and argued with the professors and read the books that they recommended. However, it appeared that this was impossible. I must pass examinations not only in Latin, but even in Greek. I could not contemplate toiling at Greek irregular verbs after having commanded British regular troops; so after much pondering I had to my keen regret to put the plan aside.[2]

Perhaps the universities of the United States are friendlier to young American Churchills. But admissions requirements and other obstacles typically stand in the way. Universities have little to lose by removing these obstacles from the path of the adult who simply wants to learn.

RELATING THOUGHT AND ACTION

"Think like men of action; act like men of thought." This dictum of Bergson's might well be a motto for actively concerned citizens. Yet it is rare to find, among the lay citizenry, persons who bear witness to the appropriateness of this sentiment. Instead one commonly finds among this group two extreme types: on the one hand, the utopians; on the other, those who, without taking thought, urge immediate action.

The utopians have solutions—neat and pretty—but they can-

[2] Winston S. Churchill, *My Early Life* (London: Thornton Butterworth, Ltd., 1930), pp. 216–17.

not describe the steps to be taken to achieve them. They point to a distant mountaintop and urge their fellow citizens to its summit; yet they cannot help cut a path through the dense wood below, nor do they know enough about the way to warn of sheer cliffs or hungry beasts. The distant peak may even prove to be a mirage; one cannot get close enough to tell. The utopians do not think like men of action; thus, they cannot relate available means to distant ends.

On the other hand, the advocates of immediate action always have a program for today and have never reflected on the cumulative effects of such actions tomorrow. They write their congressman, urging his support of a bill to raise or lower immigration quotas, but they have not considered whether a legislator ought to make his decision in response to such proddings. They maintain that, because the opposition is exerting pressure, they must do the same. But what is one to think of government by pressure? "An academic question," they say, "let's *do* something!"

Between the two extremes stands the man of practical wisdom. This man tests his thoughts by asking how they might be acted upon and tests his actions by thoughts about the consequences of his acts. When he has conjured up an idea, he asks: What would a practical man do? When he is about to rush into action, he asks: What would a wise man think?

One aim of the university is to help the actively concerned citizen become a man of practical wisdom. This does not necessarily mean that he should become less active, and certainly not less concerned. It does mean that he should become sophisticated about the relationship of means and ends. To achieve this aim, the university can take several approaches. It can lead the citizen to the men of practical wisdom: the Hamiltons, the Lincolns, the Churchills. From them the citizen can learn, by reading the Federalist Papers, the Civil War letters and speeches, or the history of the Second World War, how men of action think and how men of thought act. Another approach is the adaptation of the case method to problems of foreign affairs. Here the reader

is confronted with a problem as it is faced by the man who must make the decision, with all its complexities, uncertainties, and practical political considerations. An adaptation of the approach of the Inter-University Case Program in Public Administration to the problems of foreign policy might also yield valuable results. An experiment with the development of fictional "case-stories" as springboards to discussion, now being carried on by the American Foundation for Political Education, may prove of value as well.

INCREASING HIS ABILITY TO EDUCATE HIMSELF

Perhaps the surest sign of a man with a sound education is his ability to continue his own education, aware of his needs and able to discover the appropriate ways of meeting those needs. Sometimes he will study alone; on other occasions he will participate in organized activities. But in either case he knows what he requires, and he seeks to fulfill his needs in an independent spirit. Certain methods of adult learning can contribute much more than others to the winning of the citizens away from dependence upon purely external supports. An example is discussion leadership. The leader of the discussion must develop a capacity to guide and strengthen the conversation of the group, which has the direct result of producing in him an independent capacity to pursue his own education.[3] He learns to read better and to think more creatively. These are the very qualities he needs to enable him to pursue his own education in an independent way.

Some colleges and universities have been reluctant to put any teaching responsibility in the hands of amateurs, and certainly it must be admitted that leading a discussion is a kind of teaching. Undoubtedly there are risks in the development of educational programs in which the teaching function is left entirely to non-professionals. But there are also ways by which the university can ensure a certain minimum level of instructional quality and at the same time gain advantages which can be reaped from no other

---

[3] Of course, in a really successful group, this capacity is also developed, but to a lesser extent, among the participants.

approach. The university can exercise appropriate control over discussion programs through a review of the reading materials and the outline of the series, and by ensuring the sound selection and training of the discussion leaders. The rapidity with which such activities are spreading under the sponsorship of universities indicates that the problem of standards and appropriate supervision is being successfully met. Literally hundreds of universities now sponsor such groups, either working cooperatively with national organizations such as the Fund for Adult Education and the American Foundation for Political Education, or developing materials and training programs with their own resources.

The development of discussion leaders among the citizenry enables the university to carry out a task which it could not otherwise perform, for apparently no universities in the land are rich enough to maintain a staff of professional discussion leaders sufficiently large to lead the number of groups which an alert and aggressive administrator can establish. And, in addition, when professionals are available, the university must either charge fees high enough to meet the professional instructional cost, and, by so doing, reduce sharply the number of participants because of the price barrier, or make the program widely available through the use of nonprofessional, though competent, discussion leaders.

But most important, these programs provide opportunities for the discussion leaders to develop a high degree of skill in carrying forward their own education, making it possible for them to create within themselves, in a constantly increasing measure, the elements for unending independent learning.

CLARIFYING THE ROLE OF THE ACTIVELY CONCERNED CITIZEN

The actively concerned citizen, having both the interest and the habit of action, is the chief catalytic agent in citizen education. He induces fellow citizens to engage in the activities which interest him, and he is often responsible for persuading educators of adults that a certain program should be developed or a new course offered.

The university can serve this citizen by helping him to see clearly the role he can play and by training him to fill that role skillfully. One means of accomplishing the first aim is to educate him concerning the nature of the publics in American society. With a clear understanding of their levels of knowledge, interest, and motivation and of the correlation of these levels with factors of age, income, and education, the actively concerned citizen can visualize more sharply his own position and its opportunities. Most men tend to develop friendships and associations among people very much like themselves. They tend, as a result, to have misconceptions about those whom they do not know, either supposing them to be just like their own group or classifying them according to some other equally unreal stereotypes. A study of the various publics, and of the many varieties of persons who fall within each, would supply a corrective.

At least as important is the development of those skills which will enable him to be most effective. These skills include the ability to lead discussions, both for the purpose of learning in itself, and for the purpose of reaching agreement on some course of action; a skill in presenting ideas and opinions clearly and persuasively, orally and in writing; skill in serving effectively on boards and committees and in other leadership positions; and the ability to function politically in campaigns. Each of these skills suggests specific programs which can be devised to develop it. Training in discussion leadership has already been referred to. Courses in public speaking and in writing are offered in a variety of forms in many universities. A recent success in several institutions has been a series of meetings on "How To Be a Good Board Member." A few universities have offered programs which describe the methods of practical politics and train participants to engage in precinct work. Such a program can be nonpartisan and at the same time intensely practical.

As the university works with citizen groups, it also has the opportunity to develop leaders in less formal ways. For example, the county agricultural agent is often influential in assisting local farm organizations to select and develop the persons needed to occupy positions of responsibility. Here the training is practical and is not organized into a formal group, but it is nonetheless planned and executed with care.

All these examples of the ways in which the role of the actively concerned citizen can be clarified and his skills developed are evidence of the fact that such activities are subordinate to those, previously described, which concentrate on the development of knowledge and understanding of world affairs, for these skills are merely means for achieving ends which must be first understood and desired. Nevertheless, these practical considerations cannot be overlooked. They help make it possible for the actively concerned citizens to be effective as well as knowledgeable.

PROVIDING A RALLYING POINT

Nothing has yet been said here about the institutional place of the colleges or universities in the adult community. Yet it appears that they have a special function—this is particularly true of the evening colleges—which goes beyond their teaching of the individual, though it arises directly from that. This function is a social one; its character will depend on the temper of the times. In these times the university may serve as a bulwark for the individual against the impact of the mass society as it expresses itself through the mass media. The first task of the liberal college for adults, says C. Wright Mills, is "to keep us from being overwhelmed."[4] It can provide a rallying point for actively concerned citizens who need the supporting strength of an institution to which they can look for guidance.

The university has certain attributes which give it a special responsibility in this respect. In the first place, it has permanence

[4] C. Wright Mills, *Mass Society and Liberal Education,* in Notes and Essays, Number 9 (Chicago: Center for the Study of Liberal Education for Adults, June 1954).

and stability. It is not usually subject to the sharp changes of fortune which are the mark of most voluntary associations. The citizen feels that it will always be there! Second, while the university is nonpartisan in the narrow sense, it is very much the partisan of intelligence, the partisan of rational conversation among men. The degree to which intelligence and reason are assaulted by the media of the mass may be exaggerated by some. (In fact, it could perhaps be argued that in the United States there exists not only the most ostentatious appeal to the vulgarity of man, but, alongside it, the most vigorous current creative activity of man as artistic and rational.) Nevertheless, it is disturbing that the image of the university as a defender of intelligence in society is held by very few of the public outside. This may be due to the fact that the university—and oftentimes its adult education service especially—has confused its function and oftener serves the popular tastes for amusement than it does the creative minority, who thus look elsewhere, but usually in vain, for a rallying point.

Perhaps it needs to be said, finally, that no "public relations job" can remedy this defect where it exists. The only remedy is for the university to exhibit those qualities which are properly its own: respect for intelligence, pursuit of truth, and zeal for learning. If it does so, it can become the center of thoughtful criticism and rational invention to which the best of the actively concerned citizens will rally. Equipped with their help, the university can then hope to do its job in citizenship: the education of the attentive public, the attraction to this public of many of the inattentive, and the gradual development from both groups of an increasing number of actively concerned adults.

CHAPTER NINE

The Further Education of the Specialist

THE FORMAL preparation of the specialist in international relations occurs in the graduate departments of the universities. A review and assessment of this formal preparation is undertaken elsewhere;[1] the discussion here is limited to those aspects of the specialist's education which can be undertaken after he has achieved his full professional status either as a practicing expert in a government post or elsewhere or as a scholar and teacher in the university.[2]

Assistance in Continuing Their Own Education

The principal contribution which the university can make to the further education of specialists is to assist them in continuing their own education. In fact, it may not be an oversimplification to say that, if the university will provide convenient administrative mechanisms, the specialists will provide the educational core, for it is in the nature of this particular group that, generally speaking, they understand the need for their continuing education and know quite well where they can find the knowledge they seek.

[1] See the companion volumes to be published in this series: C. Dale Fuller, *Training of Specialists in International Relations,* and John Gange, *University Research on World Affairs.*

[2] The term "specialist" is used here in the generic sense to include both experts and scholars in a particular field. The term "scholar" is reserved for one who is learned and possesses knowledge as a result of advanced study. The term "expert" refers to one who has a special skill or useful knowledge which he has acquired by practice or experience.

The university provides its most useful service to specialists by bringing them together from within and without the university so that the experts can learn from the scholars and the scholars can, in turn, learn from the experts.

One of the well-known dangers of specialization is the consequent narrowness of perspective that it often imposes. Many experts and scholars are aware of this. Within the university, the exchange of ideas between specialized scholars in the various fields impinging upon international relations ought to occur in the regular course of scholarly fellowship. The very meaning of the university as a community of scholars contains the expectation. The adult education director is not in a position to facilitate this exchange directly, but he may be in a position to arrange meetings at which experts are brought to the university to exchange ideas with each other and with scholars in the same field. As a result of such meetings, benefits of broadening understanding will follow within the university as well as outside it.

Many universities have arranged occasions of this sort at one time or another. It would be very beneficial if a more systematic attempt could be made in a number of places along the lines of the Norman Wait Harris Institute at the University of Chicago. Here each year for a week a carefully selected group of specialists in international relations meet to discuss a topic which alternates periodically from treatment of a particular country or area (such as India or Africa, to cite two recent examples) to discussion of a general question of policy (such as technical assistance to underdeveloped areas). Experts who participate in such meetings testify to the valuable perspective and sound theoretical approach provided by the scholars, while scholars report that their own studies are illuminated by firsthand contact with the experts who must implement and accommodate policies according to the requirements of complex practical situations.

The arranging of such institutes in most universities is not often within the province of the director of extension or the dean of the evening college. Consequently it may not be amiss here to repeat that the "educator of adults" previously defined[3] is not always so obviously identified. A professor of international relations may fill the role for an occasion of this sort. The important fact is that, no matter who makes the arrangements, the university is performing a function that is appropriate to it and is of great value to the specialists involved.

Experts tend to look first to places other than the university for their own further education. In almost every case, there is a specialized institution which serves their interests in a more specific and immediate way than is possible for the university. Examples of such organizations and institutions are the Foreign Service Institute of the Department of State, the respective war colleges of the three branches of the armed services, and the Council on Foreign Relations in New York. Since scholars are regularly brought from the universities to participate in such efforts, an interchange between the experts and scholars takes place here too. But it is important that both settings should be preserved for their own distinctive values. Inevitably, and appropriately, sessions at the war colleges and the Foreign Service Institute will have an intensely practical and urgent quality. Under university sponsorship, the interchange can perhaps be expected to have a more reflective spirit. These interests balance and sustain each other. Both are required for the vigorous health of the specialist.

It should not be supposed from the foregoing that the further education of the expert occurs solely in group meetings of various types. The opposite is more typically the case. The library and the opportunities for solitary research, thought, and writing are more crucial. The very existence of the university, with its resources and its atmosphere of reflection, is in itself the fulfillment of the most crucial need in the further education of the specialist. For while exchanges of views among scholars and ex-

---

[3] See footnote 6 on p. 15.

perts may contribute substantially to the *breadth* of an individual's understanding, *depth* of knowledge is more often the product of intense and solitary study.

Serving Specialists in Adult World Affairs Education

A very different group of specialists, with a different set of problems, is found in the growing number of professionals who direct programs of world affairs education for adults. The group includes directors of local world affairs councils, regional directors of national organizations in the field, local coordinators of World Politics Programs, international relations specialists attached to extension staffs of state universities (as at the University of Wisconsin, for example), and officers of certain operating foundations (such as the Carnegie Endowment for International Peace, the Fund for Adult Education, and the World Peace Foundation). A characteristic of the group at present is that, while the functions performed by its members are highly specialized, there is no existing program of preservice professional training. The most intensive effort that has been made to train professionals for community education in world affairs was the master of arts program offered by Western Reserve University in cooperation with the Council on World Affairs of Cleveland. Despite the difficulties which prevented continuation of the program, the results of a few years' experience can be seen in the continuing active role played by participants in the work for which they were trained.

The absence of preservice training accentuates the urgency of an in-service plan of education, both in skills of programing and in the knowledge of international relations. At present, the efforts that are being made are not primarily exerted by universities, but they can be of great help. The Residential Seminars in World Affairs, which meet annually under the sponsorship of several national organizations, profit from university and college assistance. The 1955 seminar was held at Lafayette College and was enriched by the aid of members of its staff and faculty. This seminar is explicitly designed to provide an opportunity for intensive study of an issue in international relations, with complete release from the problems of administration, fund-raising, publicity, and patchwork which harry these people most of the year. A ten-day discussion of our foreign policy for Germany or for China provides a welcome and necessary change of pace.

Also there needs to be an exchange of ideas among practicing educators of adults on administrative problems and program-planning. There is much to be learned from the accumulated experience of years of effort with the attendant successes and failures. The university through its extension services can bring these people together and help them to enlighten each other. An interesting conference, which might be a preliminary step toward such meetings, was a meeting of deans, other officers, and faculty of extension divisions of seventeen universities held at the University of Minnesota in August 1955. This session was sponsored by the World Affairs Committee of the National University Extension Association. At this stage the development of a more active concern for world affairs education among university adult educators is of primary importance; the conference just referred to seems to have served this purpose. But soon there will be need for a broader exchange between university personnel and other professional nonuniversity adult educators, though perhaps on narrower geographic lines. There is abundant evidence that they can work very successfully together.

The two groups of specialists described briefly in this chapter are of very different sorts and have separate and distinct needs. There are important ways, however, in which the specialist in international relations can assist the specialist in adult world affairs education. The latter requires help in developing the substance of his educational programs. He needs sympathetic assistance in his efforts to transmit, simplify, and yet preserve the essential soundness of the material of international relations. The expert or scholar may note that the specialist in world affairs education is performing a crucial function of citizenship. It is possible for the specialist in international relations to assist in that citizenship function by bringing to bear upon it his highest knowledge and skill. Not only the inattentive, the attentive, and the actively concerned are citizens. The specialist is a citizen too. With the equipment he has as a specialist, he can, by the collaboration suggested, discharge his peculiar obligations as a citizen.

CHAPTER TEN

A Positive Program for Action

A MERICAN universities have made a substantial but highly uneven effort to provide world affairs education for adults. On every campus, at least some faculty members have taken the initiative in trying to inform their fellow citizens on international matters, but in some cases these efforts have been feeble, erratic, and marginal, while in others they have been powerful, sustained, and central. The distance between the extremes is very great.

The central aim of this book is not to make a balanced survey and appraisal of what is now occurring but to examine successful practice to discover why it succeeds. The principles inherent in outstanding programs may well be used by anyone who wishes to strengthen the work of the university in world affairs education—and perhaps in other fields as well. In this final chapter, an attempt will be made to suggest how the principles and categories developed in earlier chapters may help to provide a positive program for action in those institutions that wish to strengthen their efforts at creating in the adult public a better understanding of international relations.

Ends

All educational programs need clear aims. A generalized desire to do good is highly laudable, but to achieve results it is necessary to have practical objectives directed toward specific groups and concrete outcomes. Programs of world affairs education have often failed because their approach was too vague and general or because inadequate attention was given to identifying the audience desired. The consequences are all too evident in the courses which have few registrants, the institutes to which only the "old regulars" come, the lectures to sparsely filled halls, and the programs which have to be cancelled because they have no drawing power whatever.

When a university fails to design its programs according to some clear-cut and refined plan, but merely tries to educate people generally about world affairs, it is, in effect, adopting the approach which is characteristic of mass-media programs of communication. Insofar as the university uses such media itself (through, for example, its radio and television programs), the generalized approach may be of value. For most of its work, however, the university must develop its own distinctive methods of attack, which are not initially so obvious and direct as a mass campaign would be but which, in the long run, may have far more profound influence. These methods ordinarily imply the existence of specific objectives and the identification of groups to be served.

The specialists in international relations within the university ordinarily approach that field by many different avenues. The citizen, too, begins and develops his concern with world affairs in many different ways as it is related to his other interests. Fundamental introductory courses in the subject certainly have their place, but only as part of a far broader context of activities built around a great variety of themes and objectives. Universities have in fact developed a diversified array of approaches directed toward many different specific audiences.

Implicit in them, however, are a set of common objectives, which have been identified in chapters 6 through 9 but may be set forth in skeletonized forms as follows:

1. To help make inattentive citizens attentive.
2. To serve the continuing needs of attentive citizens for background information and understanding.
3. To encourage some of the attentive citizens to become actively concerned.

4. To serve the continuing needs of actively concerned citizens for a basic understanding of world affairs.
5. To help actively concerned citizens acquire techniques for discharging their special responsibilities more effectively.
6. To provide the opportunity for specialists to educate one another.

Each of these objectives defines both a target audience and the general nature of the result which is desired. The educator of adults, in planning a particular program, ordinarily chooses one or more of these objectives to guide him. Occasionally a program will be devoted solely to one objective, as occurs, for example, in an invitational seminar for specialists. Usually, however, programs are so constructed as to achieve two or more objectives simultaneously. Thus, a county agricultural agent may try to make farmers attentive to world affairs by developing a leadership training program for a group of actively concerned citizens; by doing so, he is combining the first and fifth objectives. Similarly, a series of lectures which is primarily focused on the second objective may be supplemented by a discussion group in which the actively concerned members of the audience have an opportunity to go into the subject more intensively with the lecturer; in this way the third and the fourth objectives are introduced.

World affairs education, like all education which aims at making people better citizens, must have as its central focus the strengthening of their basic powers as individuals. There are countless subordinate goals having to do with conveying subject matter, building an awareness of concepts, and examining critically the nature of fundamental issues and the solutions which have been proposed to specific problems. In particular cases, there may even be an effort to build a more rational adherence to established courses of action insofar as they are necessary to preserve such basic values as liberty and the democratic process. Unifying and giving meaning to all specifics, however, must be the determination to equip people to make more intelligent and moral decisions on all the issues which they must confront during their lives.

Means

The designing of a successful program requires also a careful planning of the means which are to be used. As was pointed out in chapter 5 on "The Scope of Present Services," modern universities have developed a great variety of approaches to world affairs education. Some of these are built around method. The director of a correspondence study bureau, for example, ordinarily begins with the assumption that any work which he may undertake in international relations will use correspondence study. His thinking is colored by the fact that his objectives must be attainable by the method to which he is committed. A similar orientation of viewpoint characterizes many of his colleagues, such as those who are concerned with radio, television, packaged libraries, or speakers bureaus. For the most part, however, university adult educational programs are developed around content, persons to be served, or physical facilities. The university has at least relative freedom to choose any means which may be appropriate. Also, even those units of administration which are based on method may collaborate, correspondence study being combined, for example, with other educational processes toward the achievement of some desired result.

It is a truism that the objectives of a given program should always determine the means which are to be used, but it is a truism which is often ignored in practice, for several reasons. Some educators of adults seem almost to be unaware of the range of possibilities open to them; one must infer that they keep on doing things the same way because they know of nothing else to do. Also, some methods have ardent advocates who seem to be almost unwilling to admit the possibility of any other way of doing things. In general, however, it is recognized that methods are inherently adapted to the achievement of certain kinds of goals and that, therefore, an objective defines the possible processes of education which may be used for its accomplishment. If the presentation of an ordered body of principles is desired, it is necessary to use a lecture, a film, a book, or some other similar approach. If a skill is to be taught, demonstration and practice are required. If a group wishes to examine its existing knowledge to crystallize a set of convictions or principles, it must ordinarily use discussion. To be sure, the objective does not finally determine the means; it merely limits the range of choice. There are other factors which then must be used to make a final decision, such as cost, novelty, the capacity of the leader, the wishes of the group to be taught, and the need for flexibility and variety of approach.

The task of building a successful world affairs program is, in fact, a kind of project in architecture and engineering. The man who builds a bridge across a river uses well-tested general principles, but he adapts them to the local terrain in order to achieve efficiency, economy, and beauty in a particular setting. The educator of adults must always work in the practical realm, defining specific aims for a specific audience and using means which are specifically appropriate to the local scene in which he works. The truly successful programs of world affairs education are those in which lofty and noble purposes have been coupled with a willingness to cope with practical realities.

Four Deterrents to Further Development

One of the most disturbing conclusions to be drawn from a survey of the field is that many colleges and universities do little to educate adults in world affairs.[1] The great profusion of activities described in chapter 5, taken all together, may lead one to overlook the fact that in many cities no organized program exists. This means that for a host of citizens, many of them attentive or actively concerned, educational opportunities in this field are simply unavailable. Cities in which no universities or colleges are on hand to do the job will not be touched unless the extension

[1] See Appendix (pp. 167–69).

division of the state university serves them. But in many another city there will be found a liberal arts college, a junior college, a special institute, or some other institution of higher learning. Typically, it does not engage formally in adult education in world affairs; often if it engages in any at all, the activity is sporadic and inadequately planned. An earlier chapter[2] has dealt with the appropriateness of adult education as a function of the college or university; no general assessment could overlook the fact that this issue still remains unresolved on many campuses and constitutes a major deterrent to the full development of world affairs education for the adult.

In the interviews and group discussions which have provided one of the chief sources of data for this book, university administrators and professors have frequently suggested that far more world affairs education could be made available if adequate funds and leadership could be found. It has often been declared, as well, that international relations is a controversial subject and that the university, for the sake of preserving more basic interests, should forswear any strong efforts to interest the public in the discussion of world affairs. Since progress is apparently being deterred by each of these additional factors (lack of finances, lack of instructional leadership, and the controversial nature of international relations), it is appropriate to examine each of them briefly.

The financial problem is not always as critical as it seems. Evening college deans and extension directors do find it necessary to spend a great deal of their time planning programs which provide their "bread and butter." Certain kinds of standard offerings continue year after year to produce more revenue than they consume, and, without these staples, the educator of adults usually has inadequate funds to spend on pioneering activity. Other programs, such as the Cooperative Extension Service, which are not supported by tuition fees, often have such a strong demand for their established services that they feel they cannot spend their funds on new kinds of activity. No university programs of world

[2] See pp. 73–75.

affairs education consistently make money for their sponsors. Consequently, in the hard realities of university administration, such programs receive attention only after the income-producing activities have been arranged. The difficulty often becomes, then, one of time more than one of money.

A realistic solution to the problem cannot await the day that such forms of education become money-makers. The solution will require an increased conviction of the importance of the task on the part of the administrators. But it also requires that such programs approach self-support, and a number of them are now doing so by a combination of tuition fees, contributed services of discussion leaders from the lay public, promotional assistance from organizational cosponsors, assistance from national organizations in the field, and foundation grants. This financial equilibrium depends, basically, however, on the willingness of the responsible administrator to contribute a considerable amount of his own time and attention to supervision and planning. Without that contribution, the other forms of help are hard to secure.

Frequently the financial obstacle is not a cause of failure but a convenient excuse for not trying. Administrators who feel it is desperately important to launch such a program will find ways of subsidizing it or of making it sustain itself. Those who are not so deeply concerned will tend to think that the financial risks are too great. In a recent meeting of extension directors, an attempt was made by the authors to gather data about programs of world affairs education which had been planned and prepared for launching but which finally had to be cancelled because funds could not be obtained. Not a single instance could be cited, but several cases were cited in which programs were launched with the slimmest financing and subsequently attracted support sufficient to sustain them. No one familiar with the field can claim that any financial advantages await those who enter world affairs education. On the other hand, it is no longer true, if it ever was, that the cost need be prohibitive to a determined educator of adults.

The problem of providing an adequate supply of instructional leaders is in part a matter of funds, but it is also true that the number of competent persons is in such short supply that, even if money were abundantly available, they would be hard to find. The problem is further complicated by the fact that there are relatively few positions in universities for full-time teachers of adults. Most instructional leadership must be on a part-time basis, and all too frequently the time which can be devoted to teaching adults is either added on top of a full schedule or makes up such an insignificant part of a professor's work that he must place higher priority on other demands for his time.

No university has ever completely solved the problem of securing an adequate supply of qualified instructional leadership for world affairs education, but some institutions have been more inventive than others. A first requisite is that the subject-matter departments concerned with international relations should support the adult educational programs, since such departments are usually the best source of information about competent and well-trained leaders. Scholars and experts may be drawn in on a part-time basis from many sources: the campus itself, local industry, labor unions, government departments, and countless other places. Nonprofessional lay leadership may also be used, provided adequate thought is given to designing the curriculum and to recruiting, training, and supervising the leaders. Other devices are being widely used, but they need not be detailed here. Each of the basic forms of university adult education identified in chapter 5 has developed its own way of coping with the problem.

Is world affairs education too controversial? A number of university administrators, including college presidents, deans, and adult education heads, were asked this question by the authors in late 1953 and early 1954. The replies were usually quick, interesting, and, for the most part, reassuring. One dean of a large urban university said that hardly a week passed but the administration received a complaint concerning some member of the faculty; often, but not always, political opinions were in question. But he felt that any vital university must expect this, and furthermore the complainers, except for the crackpots, were usually satisfied by a temperate and explanatory reply. Several college presidents interested in developing programs in world affairs said they would be glad to take whatever risks were involved. The head of a large university said that the university should expect to be criticized and that "the important thing about the university is that it can withstand criticism." A professor in a liberal arts college reported that increased world affairs education by the college in the community had actually reduced public criticism of the institution; prior to that time many people had felt that the campus was "too much of an ivory tower." Most of these men certainly meant what they said although not all of them had put their conviction to the test of practice.

In some institutions there seemed to be a tense division of opinion. The dean of one university spoke of his president as a "man who brooks no interference," and who is fearless in his defense of the faculty from criticism on political grounds. But an officer of the evening college at the same university reported that it had never offered anything "controversial." The town, he reported, was "very conservative, and you have to be careful." A townsman, asked for an explanation of the divergence, reported that "the faculty does not feel that the administration will stand for controversial associations or remarks by them. As for the president," he continued, "talk is cheap."

In brief, most university officers insist that controversy is the lifeblood of the university. A few do not act as if that statement were true, but those who have taken the risks have found that they and their universities could withstand the criticisms and have not regretted their courage.

The Distinctive Function of the University in World Affairs Education

In defining both ends and means, the university must always consider what its distinctive functions should be. Because it is but one of many agencies of adult education in world affairs, it has a responsibility to plan its work in such a fashion that its limited resources are most effectively used. Chapter 4 defined a set of guiding principles which might assist the process of selection and definition. These principles were derived from the practices of outstanding programs and institutions and therefore are inherent in their work. A review of each of the five principles, however, suggests ways in which some universities need to revise their present policies.

The first principle suggested that the university has an obligation to consider education as a primary purpose. Most educators of adults, and particularly evening college deans and extension directors, accept this obligation as a deep, personal conviction. There is no evidence that adult education within the university has been diverted to partisan ends or to deliberate misrepresentations. There are other ways, however, in which the principle of worthy educational standards is sometimes less successfully applied. In some institutions, the criterion of financial success appears to be more highly regarded than is the principle of educational effectiveness. This emphasis on profit is typically imposed upon, rather than willingly accepted by, the dean or director. Regardless of where the responsibility lies within the university, however, it is clear from repeated testimony that many institutions place adult education at a distinct disadvantage in comparison with other university functions, requiring of it a budgetary performance that would be considered an absurd criterion of success if applied to other educational activities. To the extent that money-making becomes paramount, education must become subordinate.

The second principle proposed that the university should emphasize educational activities which call for the use of the higher powers of the mind. The greatest problem in the practical application of this principle to world affairs education seems to be the limited size of the audience now interested in serious and intensive work. It has proved difficult for most universities to obtain registrations for an introductory course or lecture series; a consideration of what could be done beyond this beginning activity has seemed premature. But this situation is rapidly changing. In some of the larger metropolitan areas, there are literally hundreds or thousands of adults who have completed an eight- or ten-week program of reading and discussion about foreign affairs and who now seek more advanced activity. An insufficient amount of planning and forethought has been given to the great potentialities which are rapidly developing. What is needed is the conception and execution of plans which can carry the attentive citizen through successive stages of development, beginning with the less difficult and demanding and advancing to complex and exacting work. Efforts need to be made to construct such sequences, with a view both to the advancement of the attentive citizen and to the enlargement thereby of the actively concerned public.

The university needs to provide more programs of *intensive* study. One of the most sobering thoughts that confront the adult educator is the realization that so little of the citizen's time is available for study and attendance. It is not only the absolute amount that is so limiting but also the relation that the time bears to the total demands made on the adult. Home and family, job, church, and recreation will typically occupy more than nine-tenths of his time. These concerns make strong claims on his energy and attention. How can lasting effect be given to those two or three or four hours each week which can be devoted formally to education? Surely the discontinuous and occasional lecture or educational movie or discussion can rarely have permanent result.

Everything points to the urgency of persuading the attentive and actively concerned citizen to engage in a continuing and regular activity, which provides an *organized, interrelated,* and *progressing* experience. In this way one can expect that, at least occasionally in his rare moments of leisure, the citizen will reflect upon what happened last week and how it fits into his preparation for next week's session. Political education can capitalize on a special advantage it has in gaining and holding the attention and thought of the adult, namely, the daily political events which may induce the reader or listener to give attention, to weigh and judge.

Circumstances will determine how sustained the impact of the continuing activity can be; clearly it should be as sequential and regular as conditions will permit. Perhaps it will be two hours a week for twelve weeks in one case; every other week in another; occasionally opportunities will be found for a seven- or eight-day program in a residential setting in which the participant can devote all his energies and attention to his own education. The attentive citizen requires these opportunities for his development. They are even more necessary to the actively concerned, for the very reason that his attention tends to become more and more dispersed, his time less and less his own, and his personal need for complex and sustained education greater. More and more, the universities must turn their attention to the provision of such opportunities.

The third principle stated that universities should be creative in developing new forms of world affairs education. A study of current programs indicates that the universities appear to be more and more receptive to promising, even if unconventional, approaches to the education of the citizen. The wide range of activity described in chapter 5 is sufficient evidence of this fact. The notion is waning that the evening college dean or adult education director is simply the postprandial administrator of the same collection of courses offered during the day on campus.

Nevertheless, on some campuses the initiative for new approaches appears to come chiefly from outside the university, from a local citizens' group or a foundation or a national organization. There is need for more conscious and deliberate creative activity within the adult education staff. True, the staff is usually overworked and burdened with administrative detail, but the need must somehow be met. The device of a regular staff seminar, based upon some common reading and thought about educational ideas, could have this creative effect, and relieve the fatiguing effects of uninterrupted attention to problems of budget, promotion, class schedules, and the like. A self-survey conducted by a group of the faculty is another method by which scattered activities may be focused and new developments begun.[3] The university at large has resources unmatched for creative capacity, and these are not always tapped. It is good that the university is not hostile to suggestions from without, but it would be even better if the institution brought its own intelligence to bear upon these needs more often than it now does.

Adults make special demands on the inventiveness of the university. From the primary grades through college, the student constantly progresses from one stage to the next. A good elementary school, for example, can remain basically the same kind of institution over a period of years, for its student body keeps changing, and everything, no matter how long established, is new to each entering class. Not so with the adult; he may wish to turn to the university again and again for stimulus and new knowledge. He is, in a sense, always there, but he can gain nothing from the university unless it continues to offer new opportunities. He changes, his needs change, and the university must have the flexibility to provide a challenge for him each time he turns to it for a fresh educational experience. The incentive for change in curriculum and methods at any level of schooling typically comes from a desire for improvement, for perfection, and for accommodation to new social circumstances. Adult education is no exception, but, in addition, it must meet the requirement of constant inventiveness. If it does not do so, the favorite slogan of the educator of adults that "education is a life-long process" will be found to promise more than it can provide.

For the actively concerned there is a need for those more intensive efforts dealt with in the discussion of the previous principle so as to develop a truly sophisticated leadership group,

<hr />

[3] Howard E. Wilson, *Universities and World Affairs* (New York: Carnegie Endowment for International Peace, 1951).

capable of dealing familiarly with complex political issues. A number of programs are available for the upper attentive group. The pioneering need is less acute, although here too much room exists for improvement and experimentation. For the less attentive portion of the attentive public (beginning at the lower end of the scale with those who are barely distinguishable from the inattentive and stopping just short of those who have regular habits of reading and conversing about public affairs), there is need for a wide variety of pioneering attempts to educate through materials which are not beyond the present interest and aspirations of these adults. Many such attempts have been made within and without the university. They have usually had the curse of most popularization: by oversimplifying, they tend to mislead. The problem that must be solved is how to develop a plan of work and study which is attractive to the less attentive, requiring little reading and having none of the frightening trappings of university scholarship, which at the same time reveals the problems and issues of foreign affairs in all their real difficulty, and which carries the participant forward to more demanding and more rewarding subsequent study. This problem of creative curriculum building can be solved; once the terms of the problem have been set, the task becomes manageable, even though difficult.

As for the inattentive public, the main shortcoming of the university has been a failure to identify its role sharply enough to avoid the fruitless dispersal of its energy. Chapter 6 on "Arousing the Interest of the Inattentive Citizen" suggests a plan of progressive and selective development based upon the principle of interest creation described therein. Skillful steering is required if the university is to avoid the evil of either ignoring this public altogether or of exhausting itself without avail on an unselected broad assault. Charting the middle course is a pioneering challenge to the university. Once it has marked the way, it may wish to leave the channel for others to navigate.

The fourth principle proposed that the university should collaborate with the many other agencies in society which educate adults. How do present practices measure up to this principle? There is considerable evidence that the universities are better able now than in the past to work in close cooperation with a variety of community organizations and educational institutions. Even some of the large state universities, which have often encountered local community opposition to their extension activities, have developed surprisingly intimate associations with civic and educational groups, including the small colleges. Patterns of consultation and cosponsorship have frequently taken the place of jealous independence and rivalry. Some of the large universities which encounter hostility off the campus (one still hears references by local community leaders to the "octopus") might well imitate those sister institutions which have learned not to try to pre-empt adult education for themselves but have instead made better use of their resources, and actually increased their effectiveness through cooperation and sharing of responsibility.

A result of cooperative patterns of this kind should be an ability to carry some of the activities off the campus or out of the downtown center and into the neighborhoods. Universities often seem insufficiently aware of this need, which is particularly great in the large urban centers if the busy adult is to find opportunities close at hand. Incentives are rarely strong enough to induce adults to commute to work in the daytime and to commute again to study in the evening. Only a few programs now base their development on the establishment of neighborhood discussion groups and classes meeting in churches, branch libraries, homes, and other outlying meeting places. Yet this would seem to be a logical, and immensely advantageous, result of friendly working relationships with other organizations and institutions. There is evidence that, in large cities, programs which can attract a hundred adults to the downtown center or to the campus can attract a thousand if they are scattered throughout the sprawling urban and suburban metropolis. The unity of the institution must be preserved, however, even as it widens its locus; the educational program must have a center as well as a circumference. The library system of a large city, with its main library and central book collection counterbalanced by a network of branches, suggests a useful analogy. Decentralization is a possibility for only a limited number of the university's adult education activities. Where it applies, decentralization results in an effectiveness which justifies more widespread application.

The principle of cooperation with other organizations and institutions seems equally necessary in reaching each of the four publics, with perhaps somewhat less emphasis in the case of the specialists. The means of applying the principle, however, are particularly available in the actively concerned group. Those colleges and universities which have taken special interest in adult education usually have intimate ties with a number of actively concerned citizens, who provide the means of continuing cooperation with a range of community organizations and institutions. In some cases, they constitute a sort of informal "board of directors" or consultative group for the adult education program. Colleges and universities that have found it difficult to develop cooperative relationships with other institutions will find such a group an indispensable aid. Of course, the actively concerned citizen must find in the university a continuing source of education for himself; only then will he be willing to assist the university in doing the job of education in the community.

The fifth principle asserted that the university should give special consideration to the education of leaders. In practice, the universities certainly apply this principle, particularly in world affairs education. The rosters of study groups, courses, lecture series, tours, and other activities focusing on world affairs are replete with the names of community leaders, both those who have organizational posts of responsibility and those who exert a more informal type of leadership. In fact, many educators of adults even feel somewhat guilty about serving a disproportionate number of leaders. They want to reach "the public," and all they see are the "old familiar faces." There is doubtless an exaggeration here; in any group of twenty if one sees five old friends, one gets the impression of having seen a very familiar group; the new faces, being less familiar, are less sharply recalled. The university has prestige, and it attracts leaders. If the educator of adults continues to provide programs which serve their needs, he can take pride in his accomplishment.

If there is any sense in which the university tends to fall short in its education of leaders, it is with respect to their education *as* leaders. In an earlier chapter,[4] reference was made to the many ways in which leaders can be assisted to develop and perfect those skills which will enhance their values and their accomplishments as leaders. More conscious attention to this opportunity would produce rich rewards.

It is also true that the leaders who are attracted to the university are primarily the actively concerned. Yet because of their positions of leadership they hold the key to the education of a large body of the public. The deliberate attempt to identify these leaders is an urgent task for the university. If an active concern can be created and aroused within them, the further education of those they lead can thus be rapidly advanced. This problem has yet to attract the attention and determined concentration of any appreciable number of educators of adults.

The Need for Actively Concerned Leadership

When the administrative officers and professors of a university have a deep and genuine concern for world affairs education, they find ways to develop successful programs in that field. Adult education is still so new an activity at many universities that its character depends very heavily upon individual leadership. More than most other parts of the institution, adult educational divi-

4 See pp. 134–37.

sions are influenced by the capacities and interests of those who direct them. Large and stable programs of activities have not yet been permanently established at most universities. Moreover, since the program is based upon the needs and interests of the adult population, the range of activities is wide and the relative emphasis given them is constantly changing. The chief problem lies always in making the best choices among the many opportunities for action which are available and putting limited resources to the best use. Under these circumstances the program tends to reflect the values of those who administer it. The support which is given to world affairs education depends upon the extent to which the director of adult education and his staff consider it to be important.

The fourfold classification of citizens is as relevant to those who direct adult education as to those who receive it. If those who administer university extension programs are inattentive to world affairs (and some of them, most incomprehensibly, are), they will feel no need to introduce any program in that field. If they are merely attentive, they will develop such activities as appear from time to time to be appropriate. If they are actively concerned, or if they have studied international relations sufficiently deeply to be specialists, they will put world affairs education high on their list of values and will sponsor it as energetically as their resources and their other commitments permit.

A few illustrations may serve to highlight the importance of this element of personal involvement. The director of one evening college secured his own doctorate at a foreign university; it is surely not accidental that his institution sponsors a creative and imaginative program designed to build a better understanding in the United States of the country in which his alma mater is located. A dean of university extension whose interest in world affairs caused him to be chosen as a member of the National Commission for Unesco has built a program of general world affairs education for his state which has received national attention. A small college whose president has a number of international connections has developed an extraordinarily wide range of activities for the the college community and the state in which it is located. Examples could be extended without difficulty. In fact, every institution with a good program of world affairs education is an example.

The directors of adult education recognize the importance of personal commitment themselves. In the conferences and interviews on which this book is largely based, the subject came up again and again. One dean of an evening college pointed out that he felt that the central problem in the development of world affairs education was himself. As he put it, he realized he was never going to get anywhere in this field without obtaining the deliberate involvement of person after person and group after group in the building of a stronger program. His thoughts were echoed again and again by other administrators.

Those who are concerned with extending the scope of university world affairs education must often make their campus colleagues attentive and then build in them a more active concern. At one university the dean of extension has accepted the responsibility for arousing his staff to take a more active interest in international relations. He uses many means, among them an annual dinner which his division sponsors for foreign students on the campus. All the extension staff attend and, in this small and specific but very direct way, gain an added insight into international relations and a clear evidence of the concern of the dean and other institutional leaders for it. This same kind of effort can be found, to a greater or less degree, on other campuses and in many national, regional, state, and local associations of adult education, whose committees on world affairs are trying to enlarge the number of their colleagues who have an active concern for the field.

But university educators of adults are not all to be found in extension divisions, evening colleges, or other special units.

Many of them operate from other vantage points, chiefly the subject-matter departments. In some universities, however, the specialists in international relations do little or nothing to try to educate adults about world affairs. Why does this disparity in practice exist? Many members of university faculties have little or no conception of the nature or importance of adult education; they are truly inattentive to it. Others, perhaps the great majority, are attentive to university adult education and participate in it sporadically. An increasing number have developed an active and continuing concern for the education of their fellow citizens. A very few may actually be said to be specialists in adult education; usually they have at some time put in a period of service in an adult educational division.

No international relations specialist can escape the knowledge that public opinion is crucial in the shaping of national and international policy, but he may well believe that he needs to do nothing himself to help enlighten his fellow citizens. His active concern with adult education arises in the same way as does any other interest; he discovers that he cannot achieve some important goal unless he does his part in helping to spread a knowledge of world affairs. He may be moved by a desire to aid the cause of peace, to help defend the United Nations, to broaden American understanding of some foreign area or country, or to advocate or oppose a specific national policy. He may equally well be stimulated by the desire to advance his own career, to earn extra money, to broaden his range of contacts and associations, to fulfill his general responsibility as a faculty member, or to discharge his duty as a member or officer of some association to which he belongs. Whatever the pathway, the result is the same; he becomes aware of the importance of adult education and begins to undertake some specific responsibility for it.

Successful programs of university world affairs education require a knowledge of both subject matter and method. The administrators of adult educational activities and the experts in international relations must, therefore, find ways to stimulate one another so that each becomes actively concerned in the other's specialty and so that a pattern of collaboration may be worked out. The university is the only widespread institution in our society which typically contains both groups, and it is basically for this reason that the university has such an important responsibility for fostering and developing world affairs education.

Conclusion

This book has been concerned with the relationships which should exist among the three crucial terms in its title—the university, the citizen, and world affairs. These terms must always be used, not as abstract symbols, but with a sense of the variety and scope of the truth which lies behind each. Each man makes his own approach to life with a set of values and ideas that are unique to him. Each university is a highly complex social grouping with a distinctive nature and a constantly changing conception of its proper functions. The study of world affairs is never a simple or direct approach to a clear-cut subject matter; it is an effort to gain a constantly growing appreciation of the importance of an international or world-wide point of view to all areas of knowledge and experience.

Those universities that hope to use some of their resources to build a greater understanding of world affairs must approach that task with a realization of its full complexity. The understanding that most men and women have about international relations will continue to develop out of the clash of conflict and debate, and the broadening realization that world affairs are relevant to more immediate interests. Indirect learning will continue to be stimulated by particular circumstances and by the influence of mass media of communication. It is essential, however, to avoid both the apathy and the instability which have characterized public opinion on foreign affairs in the past, and to enlarge that group in our population which has a sufficient perspective to enable it to temper immediate impulses by a consideration of long-run values and to bring to the solution of specific problems the lessons which have been learned through past experience. This end can be achieved only by the development of programs of education which aim at the enlargement of the number of people in our society who have a continuing, informed, and balanced viewpoint toward world affairs.

Sources

THE MATERIAL for this book has been drawn from many sources. In addition to the published literature in the field, the authors have had access to the unpublished self-study reports of many universities and colleges prepared in cooperation with the Carnegie Endowment for International Peace. The authors have also conducted interviews with a number of leaders inside and outside the universities, and have profited from conferences of adult educators set up especially for the purpose of examining the university's function in adult world affairs education. So many individuals have been involved by these various means that it now appears impossible to mention them by name. The authors are immensely grateful for the contributions they have received through these interviews and conferences.

The self-study reports sponsored by the Endowment covered the whole range of university activity in world affairs. Of the fifty-seven institutions which had concluded their surveys at the time of completion of this volume, thirty-one have no highly organized adult education programs in world affairs; their participation is limited to faculty lectures to community organizations at irregular intervals on a wide variety of subjects. Twelve institutions reported activities somewhat more extensive, but either have no organized adult education program, or, in case they do, have no conscious policy of regularly offering adult education in world affairs. Ten schools reported organized adult education activities with a conscious policy of continuing education of some sort in world affairs. Two institutions reported that they give emphatic attention to adult education about world affairs. Two institutions could not be included in any of the above categories because their administrative organization precludes a separation of adult educational activities from the regular program of the undergraduate student body.

These fifty-seven institutions do not necessarily provide a representative sample of American universities and colleges as a whole. Their reports do suggest two generalizations, however, which in all probability hold true of the groups as a whole. First, the small liberal arts colleges are the least likely to have an organized program of adult education; and women's colleges are, within that category, the least likely of all. Thus, of the thirty-one institutions least active, sixteen were small liberal arts colleges, and, of these, nine were women's colleges, while none of these institutions appeared in the two most active categories. Second, the likelihood of active adult education in world affairs increases with the size, complexity, and public character of the institution; thus nine of the twelve institutions which were characterized as either having a "conscious policy" or giving "emphatic attention" are state universities; the remaining three are also large and complex.

The authors conducted approximately a hundred and ten interviews. Each usually lasted several hours, and was directed toward a full consideration of those issues most interesting to the interviewed person, rather than toward a statistical compilation of brief replies to specific questions. The interviews were designed primarily for the purpose of exploration and exchange of ideas. Discussions took quite different directions, depending upon the interests and experience of the man interviewed and the character of his institution. These were some of the questions discussed: What does your institution do in world affairs education? How is it organized to carry on this work? What important projects are going on elsewhere? What do you consider the major obstacles to more successful world affairs education? How important is it? Is world affairs education too controversial? How do you answer criticism? What are the most important things the citizen needs to know about world affairs?

The persons interviewed included administrators and faculty members in thirty-one institutions of higher learning. Among them were sixteen college and university presidents, twelve deans or directors of adult education activities, and over fifty persons in other administrative posts or in faculty positions in political science, history, government, and other fields.

For a perspective on the university from knowledgeable sources outside it, interviews were held with leaders in public affairs education, a leading radio network executive, present and former members of the Department of State, members of the Cooperative Extension Service of the Department of Agriculture, and other persons who are part of the group designated as the "actively concerned."

These interviews provided a great deal of information and a number of helpful suggestions which have found their way into the book.

The National University Extension Association convened a conference on The University and World Affairs Education at the University of Minnesota in August 1955 at which an early draft of this book served as a working paper. Leaders in adult education from seventeen universities in all parts of the United States participated in an intensive two-day discussion of the major issues. In similar fashion the Association of University Evening Colleges sponsored a meeting of deans and other officers of some of the larger urban evening colleges in October 1955. Both of these meetings provided healthy and valuable critical comment.

The authors are particularly indebted to Gabriel Almond, Robert J. Blakely, Mary Louise Collings, Maurice F. X. Donohue, Robert A. Goldwin, Morton Gordon, J. R. Kidd, Malcolm S. Knowles, Joseph L. Matthews, George W. Overton, George Parkinson, Roy R. Tompkins, Louise Leonard Wright, and Quincy Wright. Each of them has read the manuscript and made helpful comments which resulted in many improvements in the text. A similar acknowledgment should be made of the usefulness of the conversations and correspondence with the authors of the other volumes in this series.

Howard E. Wilson has performed admirably and well the difficult task of a general editor of the series. His careful and precise comments have been gratefully received at every stage of preparation. He has been most helpful in clarifying the text and criticizing its main ideas.

James Crimi's unpublished study of the adult education activities of eighteen liberal arts colleges provided valuable information.

The original stimulus and much of the support for the study came from the Carnegie Endowment for International Peace. The officers and executive committees of the Adult Education Association, the National University Extension Association, and the Association of University Evening Colleges have been unfailingly helpful. Thanks are also due to the Carnegie Corporation of New York for its support and particularly to Miss Florence Anderson, secretary of the Corporation, for her interest and assistance.

Mention should also be made of the research assistance of H. Dicken Cherry and Allan O. Pfnister, the editorial assistance of Miss Mildred Herrod, and the patient and accurate secretarial service of Mrs. Leonard Gerin.

Although the authors are finally responsible for what appears in this volume, they are fully aware of the sizable debt they owe their many colleagues who have assisted in one or another of the ways mentioned above.

Bibliography

MUCH HAS been written about the world affairs education provided by universities for adults, but a great deal of this writing consists of news notes about proposed or existing programs, descriptions of particular methods or materials, and analyses of the work undertaken by individual units or services, such as the Cooperative Extension Service, the evening colleges, or the correspondence study bureaus. The reader who is interested in building up a knowledge of what is now going on must examine many periodicals, bulletin series, and proceedings of conferences and conventions.

The following brief list of references has been selected to provide a sampling of this descriptive material from the sources most readily available to general readers. The few available analytical sources are also included. The literature of such related subjects as international relations, higher and adult education, and public opinion is omitted since excellent bibliographies on these subjects are available.

ADAM, THOMAS R. *Education for International Understanding.* New York: Institute of Adult Education, Teachers College, Columbia University, 1948.

BROWN, GILES T. "Two Minutes Are Not Enough!" *Junior College Journal,* October 1954, pp. 75–82.

CHERRINGTON, BEN M. *Methods of Education in International Attitudes.* New York: Bureau of Publications, Teachers College, Columbia University, 1934.

COHEN, BERNARD. C. *Citizens in World Affairs.* Princeton, N.J.: Center of International Studies, Princeton University, 1953.

CORY, ROBERT H., JR. *Communicating Information and Ideas about the United Nations to the American People.* New York: Carnegie Endowment for International Peace, 1955.

GRUMMAN, RUSSELL A. *University Extension and Action.* Chapel Hill: University of North Carolina Press, 1947. Pp. 91–105, 125–29.

HOLT, GEORGE C. "The Conference on World Government," *Journal of Higher Education,* May 1946, pp. 227–35.

HUSZAR, GEORGE B. DE (ed.). *New Perspectives on Peace.* Chicago: University of Chicago Press, 1944.

LOOMIS, CHARLES P., and OTHERS. *Rural Social Systems and Adult Education.* East Lansing: Michigan State College Press. Pp. 69–72, 137–43, 244–70.

MITCHELL, RUTH CRAWFORD. "The National Rooms at the University of Pittsburgh and International Understanding," *Higher Education,* Oct. 15, 1950, pp. 37–40.

"Programing for World Affairs: A Symposium," *Adult Leadership,* July-August 1953, pp. 1–32.

"Report of the Committee on World Affairs," *Proceedings of the Fortieth Annual Meeting of the National University Extension Association,* XXXVIII (1955), 128–31. (See also *Proceedings of the Thirty-eighth Annual Meeting of the National University Extension Association,* XXXVI [1953], 133.)

"Report on Oversea Workshops: A Symposium," *Journal of Educational Sociology,* December 1952, pp. 146–92.

ROCKWOOD, RAYMOND O. "How College and Community Work Together," *Journal of Educational Sociology,* December 1946, pp. 221–36.

SHARP, MARGARET M. "An Experiment with Community Forums," *Adult Education Bulletin,* December 1947, pp. 43–44.

SILLARS, ROBERTSON. "Education for International Understanding: A Report of a Survey," *Adult Education Journal,* April 1949, pp. 91–98.

STUHLER, BARBARA. "State Organization Service," *Proceedings of the Thirty-ninth Annual Meeting of the National University Extension Association,* XXXVII (1954), 16–18.

UNIVERSITY OF MINNESOTA CENTER FOR CONTINUATION STUDY. *The University and World Affairs Education.* A Report of a Conference Sponsored by the Committee on World Affairs of the National University Extension Association, Aug. 28–30, 1955. Minneapolis: The Center, 1955.

WILSON, HOWARD E. *Universities and World Affairs.* New York: Carnegie Endowment for International Peace, 1951.

WRIGHT, QUINCY. "The Universities and the World Order," *Bulletin of the American Association of University Professors,* Spring 1947, pp. 43–54.

Index

Ability to face and assess facts, 113–14, 130

Acheson, Dean, 111

Action, overt, as motivator of interest in world affairs, 84–85

Actively concerned citizen
characteristics of, 126–27
chief catalytic agent in citizenship education, 135–36
role in formation of policy, 39, 43–44
skills, development of, 136
and task of adult education, 35–36
university services to, 129–38

Adam, Thomas R., 91

Adult education
in American cultural history, 45
organization of, 46–53
organization of services within university, 75–78
as a university function, 73–75

Adult Education Association of the U.S.A., 169

Adult education programs
categories of, 50
common elements in, 51–52
differences in, 52
regular university courses offered in, 62
shifting emphasis in, 52–53
university, 53–54

Adult education in world affairs
lack of programs of, in many communities, 149–50
pioneering opportunities in, 125
tasks of, 28–30, 43–44

Adult political education
fundamental propositions in, 104–12

Adult political education—*Continued*
plan required for, 105–8

Adults' demands on creativeness of university, 157

Advocates of immediate action among actively concerned, 133

Age, and attention to world affairs, 80

Alabama College, program service for groups, 70

Alabama, University of, Slavic Areas Program, 124

Almond, Gabriel, 79–82, 87, 88, 98, 169

Alumni, educational programs designed for, 69

American Association for the United Nations, 50, 64, 127

American Foundation for Political Education, 50, 134, 135

American Friends Service Committee, 127

American Legion, 127, 128

American-Scandinavian Foundation, 48

American Veterans Committee, 127

Americans for Democratic Action, 127

Ancestry, and interest in world affairs, 94–95

Anderson, Florence, 169

Apathy of inattentive citizen, 79

Area study, 62, 124

Ascham, Roger, 23

Associated Countrywomen of the World, 68

Association of University Evening Colleges, 168, 169

Attentive citizen
characteristics of, 112–13
goals for education of, 113–22
role of, in formation of policy, 39, 43–44

Attentive citizen—*Continued*
and task of adult education, 34–35,
104–25
university programs for, 123–25
Attributes of university, 137–38
Audience to be reached, 26, 28, 33–34,
79, 146. *See also* Actively concerned
citizen, Attentive citizen, Inattentive citizen, and Specialist
Authority, as strategy in interesting inattentive citizen, 88–89

Bailey, Thomas, 43
Baker, Vincent, 106
Bergson, Henri, 132
Blakely, Robert J., 169
Bologna, University of, 47
Bryce, James, 40
Burke, Edmund, 37

California, University of, and patterns
of organization of adult educa-
tion services, 76
California, University of, at Los An-
geles, 102
Capacity for critical judgment, 114–15,
130
Carnegie Corporation, 169
Carnegie Endowment for International
Peace, 48, 142, 167
universities and world affairs pro-
gram of, xi–xiii
Case method, adaptation of, to prob-
lems of foreign affairs, 133–34
Cherry, H. Dickson, 169
Chicago Council on Foreign Relations,
124
Chicago, University of
course on "Labor's Stake in World
Affairs," 101
Norman Wait Harris Institute, 65,
140
University College, 124
University College, Basic Program of
Liberal Education for Adults,
109–10
Churchill, Winston, 132, 133

Cincinnati, and effect of mass campaign in, 25–26, 29, 87
Citizen role in foreign policies compared with role in domestic policies, 41–42
City College of New York, associate in
arts program on world affairs, 125
Clarifying role of actively concerned
citizen, university's role in, 135–37
Cleveland Council on World Affairs,
142
Clubs and associations, specialized program services for, 70
Colgate University, Conference on
American Foreign Policy, 64, 130–
31
Collaboration between educators of
adults and experts in international
relations, 7, 143–44
Collaboration of university with other
agencies, 58–60, 100–102
Collings, Mary Louise, 169
Columbia University, American Assem-
bly, 65
Committees on world affairs in adult
education associations, influence of,
163
Community development and involvement of inattentive citizen in
world affairs, 91–92
Complexity of foreign policy, 41–43
as pervasive theme, 116–17
Complexity of subject and interest in,
theory of relationship of, 85–86
Concentrated educational offerings for
actively concerned, need for, 130
Consultative or reference bureaus, 72
Controversial nature of international
relations, 150, 152–53
Cooperative Extension Service, 4, 48,
61, 67–69, 76, 98–99, 150
Correspondence study programs, 64
Council on Foreign Relations, 48, 126,
141
Course sequences designed for adults,
62
Creativity, need for, in program build-
ing, 156–57
Crimi, James, 169
Curtiss-Wright case, 41

Decentralization of university's adult education activities, value of, 159–60

Decisions, intelligent and moral, helping citizen make, 147–48

Denver, University of, Social Science Foundation, lecture series on world affairs, 123

Department of Agriculture, 68
Federal Extension Service, 168

Department of State, 141, 143, 168

Deterrents to further development of adult world affairs education, 149–53

Direct and indirect learning, 22–23

Direct and specialized approaches, 28–30

Discipline, as a mode of analysis, 18–19

Discussion leadership, and increasing ability to educate self, 134–35

Donohue, Maurice F. X., 169

Education
and attentiveness to world affairs, 81–82
coordinate with other functions in adult education programs, 49
formal, and adult interest in world affairs, 94
of leaders, 58–59, 160–61
primary purpose in adult education programs, 48–49
primary purpose of university, 54–55, 154
subordinate function in adult education programs, 49

Education of Henry Adams, The, 22–23

Educator of adults
defined, 15, 141
and importance of concern for world affairs education, 161–62
and inattentive citizen, 82–86
as pioneer, 57
role of individual, in world affairs education, 60
task of, 9–31

Elites, as motivator of interest in world affairs, 90–91

Employment, and interest in world affairs, 95

English-Speaking Union, 48

Enlarging actively concerned public, 127–28

Exchange of visitors, 13

Executive, role of, in foreign policy, 41, 43

Facts Forum, 127

Farm and Home Week, 68

Fear, as motive for interest in world affairs, 95

Federal Union, 127

Film-discussion program, 124

Finances, problem of, in university adult education in world affairs, 150–51

Florida, University of, pattern of adult education services, 77

Focus and balance, need for, in organization of university adult education, 75–78

Foreign affairs. See World affairs

Foreign Policy Association, 48, 126

Foreign policy, relationship of, to ends of man, 109

Foreign Service Institute, 141

Foreign students and visitors, organized services for, 71–72

Framework of adult education agencies, 47–48

Freedom House, 48

Fund for Adult Education, 135, 142
"World Affairs Are Your Affairs," sponsored by, 124

Gerin, Mrs. Leonard, 169

Gillispie, Charles C., 58

Goals
for attentive citizen's education, 113–22
of educational programs, 145–48
limited value of generalized approaches to, 146
and means, relationship between, 148–49
of university adult education, 6

Goals—*Continued*
of world affairs education, disagreement regarding specific, and methods, 7
Goldwin, Robert A., 169
Gordon, Morton, 169
Great Decisions Program, 100, 124
Group processes, as motivator of interest in world affairs, 92–93

Hamilton, Alexander, 38, 40, 133
Harvard University, 77
Herrod, Mildred, 169
Higher mental powers
emphasis on use of, in university education, 55–56
need for, in adult world affairs education, 54–56

Illinois, University of, 130
institute for union members, 100–101
Inattentive citizen
identification of, for purpose of creating interest, 96–97
making, attentive, 103
media appropriate to, 87–88
profile of, 79–82
role of, in formulation of policy, 39
strategies for interesting, 86–93
and task of adult education, 34
university and, 97–102
Income, and attentiveness to world affairs, 80–81
Increase of information, 86–88
Increasing actively concerned citizen's ability to educate self, 134–35
Increasing knowledge of actively concerned citizen, 129–32
Indiana University, *Selected Films for World Understanding,* 66
Indirect learning, and growth of international understanding, 24–25
Individualized learning, dominant in world affairs education, 46
Indochina situation, example of complexity of foreign policy, 120
Inseparability of foreign and domestic questions, examples of, 110–12

In-service training for specialists in world affairs education, 142–43
Insight into pervasive themes in foreign affairs, 115–20, 130
Intensive study, need for more programs of, 155
Interest groups as motivator of inattentive citizen, 89–90
Interest in world affairs, creation of, 93–97
International Cooperation Administration, 72
International Farm Youth Exchange, 72
International Press Institute, survey of Americans' knowledge of world affairs, 10
International relations
approaches to subject of, 15–24
concern of specialists with definition of, 16–20
seen as discipline of synthesis, 19–20
as separate discipline, 17–18
Inter-University Case Program in Public Administration, 134
Introductory course in international relations, 146
for adult citizen, 106–8
for college student, 105–6
Iowa Nurses Association, 99
Iowa, University of, Center for Continuation Study, 99
Isolationism of immigrants to the United States, 12

Jefferson, Thomas, 40
Junior Chamber of Commerce, 50

Kennan, George, 120
Kidd, J. R., 169
Kirk, Grayson, 18
Knowledge, direct, of foreign countries, 11–12
Knowledge of world affairs, Americans', 10–15, 79–82
Knowledge and understanding, values of, for their own sake, 85
Knowles, Malcolm S., 169

Kriesberg, Martin, study of knowledge of world affairs, 11, 79

Lafayette College, 142
Laves, Walter H. C., 114
Leadership
    educational, variety of ways of coping with problem of, 150, 152
    need for actively concerned, 161–65
League of Women Voters, 50
Lectures, 123
Legislative, role of, in foreign policy, 41
Liberal education
    distinguished from vocational training, 108, 109
    focus of, 108–9
    indispensable to complete citizenship, 108–10
    integrated program of, for adults, 109–10
    international relations in adult programs of, 124–25
Limits of American power, as pervasive theme, 117–18
Lincoln, Abraham, 133
Lippmann, Walter, on public opinion, 27, 30, 37, 87
Literary Digest, 13

Manning, C. A. W., 22
Mass campaigns, 24–27
    limitations of, as educational devices, 26, 28
    possibilities of, as stimulator of direct learning, 29–30
Mass media
    and learning about world affairs, 12–13, 24–25
    low level of effect of, 27
Matthews, Joseph L., 169
Maugham, Somerset, 122
Means, in designing adult world affairs programs, 148–49
Media, need to use, appropriate to inattentive citizen, 87–88
Methods used by university to interest inattentive citizen, 98–102

Miami University, Alumni College, 69
Miami, University of, service to community, 63
Michigan State University
    "Community Adventures in World Understanding" and "Christmas Adventure in World Understanding," 71–72
    Continuing Education Service, 76
Michigan, University of, 130
    Television Hour, 66
Midwest Seminars on American Foreign Policy, 130
Mills, C. Wright, 137
Minnesota, University of, 130, 143, 168
    State Organization Service, 70
Morality and national interest, as pervasive theme, 118–19
Motives for interest in world affairs. *See* Interest
Mount Holyoke College, Institute on United Nations, 65

National Association of Educational Broadcasters, 65
National Commission for Unesco, 162
National Opinion Research Center, 25–26, 87
National University Extension Association, 64, 143, 168, 169
Nebraska, University of, 67
Newspaper, as instrument of education, 27, 29–30
New York University
    Division of General Education, 76–77, 109
    tours, 72–73
North Carolina, University of, Annual Conference on World Affairs, 65
Northwestern University, Reviewing Stand, 65

Objectives. *See* Goals
Obstacles to adults entering university, 132
Occupational grouping, and attention to world affairs, 81

Orange Coast College, weekly meetings on world affairs, 123
Oregon Division of University Extension, 76
Oregon State College, Institute on the Far East and World Affairs, 124
Oregon State System of Higher Education
General Extension Division, 100
Institute of International Affairs, 70–71
Oregon World Affairs Council, 100
Organization and association, distinction between, 47
Overton, George W., 169

Paris, University of, 48
Parkinson, George, 169
Pennsylvania State University, Institute on World Affairs and International Cooperation, 64–65
Pfnister, Allan O., 169
Pioneering in world affairs education, 55–56
Pittsburgh, University of, nationality rooms, 63
Plato, 23
Popular opinion. *See* Public opinion
Portland *Oregonian,* 100
Preservice professional training for adult world affairs educators, lack of, 142–43
Principles
of effective learning, 26–29
guiding, for university, 53–59
Production and publication of educational materials, 71
Programs
to aid local communities, 66–67
to aid special occupational groups, 67–69
See also Adult education programs, University adult education
Progression in learning experiences, and interest in world affairs, 85–86
Provision of instructional materials, 66
Public
implications of segments of, 33–36

Public—*Continued*
and representative government, 36–39
roles of, in formation of policy, 39, 43–44
See also Actively concerned citizen, Attentive citizen, Inattentive citizen, Specialist
Public opinion, 32–44
on foreign policy, factors affecting, 40–44
role of, as guide in educational programs, 32–33, 43–44
role of, in conduct of foreign affairs, as pervasive theme, 119–20
Purpose
centralization of, 43
effect of intensity of, on learning, 23
relation of education to primary, 48–52

Radio programs, 65
Rallying point, university's function in providing, 137–38
Reactions of educators to citizen inattentiveness to world affairs, 82–84
Readiness of responsive public for education, 104, 112
Reading and discussion, 123–24
Recognition and use of adult experience, 106–8
Regional variations in attention to world affairs, 81
Relating thought and action, 132–34
Residential Seminars in World Affairs, 142–43
Resources for understanding world affairs, 2–3
Responsibility
as motivator of interest in world affairs, 84
of university for developing world affairs education, 165–66
Role of mature American in shaping foreign policy, 7
Role performance, as motivator of interest in world affairs, 96
Roles of mature American, 1–3
integration of, 6

Rural-urban differences in attention to world affairs, 81
Rutgers University, 70

Satisfaction, lack of, for beginner's interest in world affairs, 85–86
Schools and universities, efforts of, to spread knowledge of world affairs, 13–15
Secrecy, in foreign policy, 42
Self-surveys, xi–xiii, 167
Sex, and attentiveness to world affairs, 80
Shaw, George Bernard, 24
Short course and conference programs, 64
Skills, development of, for actively concerned citizen, 136
Smith-Lever Act, 67
Social need, university's responsibility to meet, 57
Social pressure and interest in world affairs, 95
Source of actively concerned citizens, 128–29
Speakers bureaus, 70–71
Specialist, 35, 36
    further education of, 139–44
    responsibility of, in educating adults, 163–65
    role in formation of policy, 39, 43–44
    and scholar, university's function in interchange between, 139–40
Specialists in adult world affairs education, need for in-service training of, 142–43
Specialized institutions for specialists, 61
Spencer, Herbert, 28
Sponsorship of leagues or competitions, 72
Standards, maintenance of, 55–56
State Department, 13, 118, 141
State University Teachers College, New Paltz, New York, 64
Strategies for interesting inattentive citizen, 86–93
Sutherland, George, 41

Synthesis
    as base for enlargement of understanding, 30
    discipline of international relations, a, 19-20
    as focus for citizen education, 20–22

Television programs, 65–66
Theoretical understanding of international relations, 120–21, 130
Theory
    of international relations, 122
    purpose of, 121–22
Tompkins, Roy R., 169
Tocqueville, Alexis de, 40
Tours, 72–73
    as motivator of interest in world affairs, 99–100
Tradition of adult educational service, need for, 77–78
Truman, Harry S., 43

United Nations, 25–26, 64, 73, 164
United World Federalists, 48, 127
University
    and actively concerned citizen, 129–38
    and attentive citizen, 113–25
    function of, in world affairs education, xi–xiii, 45–59, 153–61
    and inattentive citizen, 97–102
    service of, to specialists in mass media, 101–2
    and special activities for community, 63–64
    sponsorship of discussion programs, 134–35
University adult education
    categories of programs in, 53–54
    common core of programs in, 60–61
    evolution of, 61, 73–74
    opposition to, 74–75
    patterns of future programs of, 78
    programs most frequently found in, 61–73
    services of, 60–78
    specially designed courses in, 62–63
    status of, 73

University adult education—*Continued*
  in world affairs, general assessment
    of, 145–66
University and World Affairs Education Conference, 168
Utopians among actively concerned, 132–33

Virginia, University of, 67
Voluntary associations, and adult education in world affairs, 13, 20–21, 89–90

Walpole, Horace, 32
War colleges of armed services, 126, 141
Warfare, potential role of, in formation of foreign policy, 42–43
Wars, as source of knowledge about world affairs, 12
Washington, George, 42
Washington, University of, 67
Weekly meetings, 123
Western Reserve University, 142
Wilson, Howard E., 169

Wilson, Woodrow, 40
  and Fourteen Points, 118
Wisconsin, University of, 130, 142
  program services of, to groups, 70
Women's International League for Peace and Freedom, 127
World affairs councils, 50
World affairs education
  need for, 9–10
  and other aspects of political education, 110–12
  reasons for importance of, for adults, 14–15
  role of universities in, 3–5, 45–59
  See also Adult education in world affairs, Liberal education, University, University adult education
World Peace Foundation, 142
World Politics Program, 123–24, 126, 142
Wright, Louise Leonard, 169
Wright, Quincy, 169
Wriston, Henry M., 121–22

Zimmern, Sir Alfred, 119

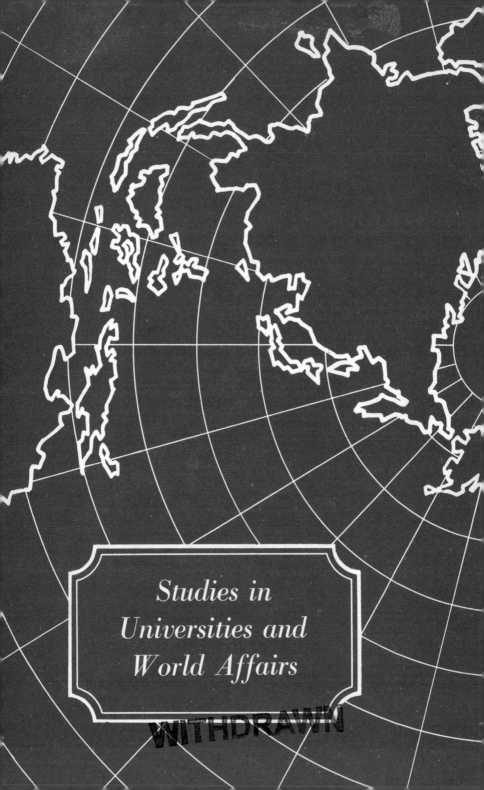

Studies in
Universities and
World Affairs